MY BEAUTIFUL
FAITH

MY BEAUTIFUL
FAITH

by Jill McDowell

Printing in the United States of America
First Printing, 2024
ISBN 979-8-218-46492-9
Published by Jill McDowell
Printed by IngramSpark
Ingram Content Group, Inc.
1 Ingram Blvd.
La Vergne, TN 37086
www.IngramSpark.com

iv

My Beautiful Faith is dedicated to the people who have guided and nourished my faith over the years. My grandmother, Lola, who planted seeds of love and shared words of wisdom wrapped in her faith. My father, who, without his leading by example, I would not be the strong woman of faith I am today. My son, Patrick, who is not only a blessing, but also a loving reminder that love is patient and kind by his thoughtfulness and kindness.

Lennis

The man is a success who has lived well, laughed often, and loved much; who has gained the respect of intelligent men and the love of children; who has filled his niche and accomplished his task; who leaves the world better than he found it, whether by an improved poppy, a perfect poem, or a rescued soul; who never lacked appreciation of earth's beauty or failed to express it; who looked for the best in others and gave the best he had.

—ROBERT LOUIS STEVENSON

*L*ennis was a carpenter by day and a handy man by night. Throughout our thirty years together, I never recall a time that he refused to help a single soul. He wouldn't think twice about helping a friend or family member no matter what the task. I always admired that about Lennis, and considered his sharing spirit to be rare and valued.

We rarely discussed our faith early on in our marriage, but I always thought that someone with such a generous soul and helping hand must certainly believe in God.

He grew up in a religious home environment, and became rebellious in his beliefs as an adult, as during that time he was forced to believe.

I never understood how someone could waver in their faith in God, but I was never forced to believe so I can't understand those thoughts.

Later as he came closer to death, he accepted Jesus as his savior, and recited the Sinner's Prayer while in the hospital. He had told me that he accepted Jesus as his Lord and Savior a couple of times earlier in his life. He recited the prayer once at a Billy Graham conference and another time before that. He wanted heaven's door to be wide open and I believe that with this simple prayer it was.

My faith remains strong and is reinforced with healthy roots knowing that my husband now has a glorious new body and everlasting life. You see, when you believe in Jesus and that he died on the cross to release your sin, and you ask forgiveness for your sin, your ticket to everlasting life is waiting for you when that time comes. It's sometimes difficult for a person to understand this, but once your faith develops, it becomes your truth. It's a glorious thing when this happens!

It's taken me years to understand the importance of

the sinner's prayer and the impact it has over our next eternal life, heaven.

Think of heaven as a well-run and organized business. One would imagine that it would have to have some form of structure to be a place called heaven. I can only imagine, and not really ponder just how magnificent it will be. We get so wrapped up in our day-to-day living here on earth, we forget to realize that there's a better life after this one.

Through my faith, I know heaven is real.

I sometimes place my focus on these thoughts, but I must warn you, once you do begin thinking this way, the world in which you live will look much different. I sometimes think it feels like I'm not of this world. In reality, when your faith grows and you put your trust in God, each day thoughts like this are not uncommon. It's okay to feel this way.

One thing I've learned as I get older is that faith grows when you seek it. Putting your trust in something that you cannot touch or feel can be challenging, but if you remain determined to keep the faith, you will experience a peace and joy unlike anything you've ever experienced!

There's no drug, amount of money, or earthly potion that can duplicate the feeling that a born-again Christian feels.

A New Path

W e are each born into this world and loved by the same God. Every tiny new babe who arrives has a heavenly father who loves him or her with all his might. Each of us travels a different path. Sometimes we follow the same worn-out path, while other times we create a new one. Both paths are lined with free will.

I've learned to realize how this is an amazing gift given to us from God. This gift can't be seen or heard, and it bases its decisions strictly on your instruction. Your free-will decisions can easily be taken advantage of and abused. The outcome is always determined by your instruction. Most of us know when we're taking advantage of our free will, and we also know that there's a price to pay when we do. As I read the Bible it becomes clear to me how this same free will lined the path for all that lived during that time just as it does today.

I can look back and recall how the decisions that I made determined the path that I chose. Most of the time it's been rocky and uneven, I was stumbling and tripping, and then falling, only to get up, pat myself off and start over again. It was exhausting! My life felt as though it was never complete and as though something important was always missing. It took me many years to understand and to learn what was missing. This is what I'll share with you!

This book reveals my story and what I've done to develop my faith and nourish its growth. People say that this form of spiritual growth is different for everyone. I'm not in disagreement with that, but I don't agree with it either.

Is that even possible, you ask? I believe so. Each of us is developing our trust in God each day, but we may not recognize it when it's happening. God has a supernatural way of teaching us this. Surprisingly, the ups and the downs have helped to cultivate and nourish my faith. These teachings were learned as my faith grew and not so much when I was young, but later in life after I had my born-again moment. Most of all I've learned that even in my darkest of times, when you put your trust in God, He will never let you down.

If any of you lacks wisdom, let him ask God, who gives generously to all without reproach, and it will be given him. But let him ask in faith, with no doubting, for the one who doubts is like a wave of the sea that is driven and tossed by the wind. For that person must not suppose that he will receive anything from the Lord; he is a double-minded man, unstable in all his ways.

—JAMES 1:5–8

The other night just before falling asleep my mind began pondering thoughts of how rich and complete my life is compared to how it once was. Those thoughts are always surrounded with miraculous and supernaturally unexplainable feelings that are hard for me to put into words. I will try to explain.

When one puts their trust in God, and lets go of the habit of leaning on themselves and others around them, they develop a strong sense of peace that feels euphoric and supernatural. When you relinquish this trust, then and only then your soul fills with joy. I haven't always felt this strongly about my faith, and it sometimes feels like I know something that others do not. *A Jill secret*, I thought.

Although I've always been a believer, until I began reading the Bible my heart and soul were not fully capable of understanding the abundant and constant love that comes from above. When you think of heaven you can't help but think it's a long way off. It's not. Heaven is right next to you. When you are a believer, Heaven is in you. These heavenly thoughts offer what I call soul satisfaction.

Knowing that this unconditional love and having the

knowledge that God is always with you no matter how dire the situation never wavers and always stands firm. When your mind allows these thoughts to run free and you develop this sense of trust, you become closer to God. When you become close to God your thoughts and ideas about life become more positive. You're happier. You're not hung-up on things that once challenged you. You've been set free.

How on earth did I ever get to where I'm at today? You hear stories all the time about how someone becomes a born-again Christian. For me it was a bit different than most. Most people recall the exact moment when they turned their heart over to God. I really don't remember that moment. It was more of an extended moment that turned into hours, and then days, months, years.

It's ironic how once you begin walking on this faith journey, the people, places, and things that come into your life seem to show up at just the right time. At least this is what I've found. I call these moments *divine timing*. Sometimes if you're not looking, you'll miss them. Believe it or not, they are present each and every day. From the moment you wake until the time you go to bed. When you start to look for them they appear more. When your faith grows, these moments expand and explode and exceed any ideas, thoughts or outcomes you could ever conjure up on your own.

Being human can bite you in the butt! That's right, after everything that I just said, you must know that life will not be easy. There will be tragedies, deaths, sadness, disappointments, and dismay. However, when your heart turns to Jesus, the bad things will not overcome you as they once did, and you will fall upon your trust and faith. Both will gently guide you through until the next bad thing happens. These life moments, as tragic as they may be, will be filled with peace and understanding that, as a believer, He will and always will have your back.

I wish that I could tell you that when you walk in faith bad things won't happen. Unfortunately that's not the case. In fact it may feel like when you walk in faith bad things pop up even more. When bad things do happen however, and when you walk in faith your attitude is completely different than a person that doesn't. There is a difference. If a person never takes that walk they will never understand the difference. However, if you put your trust in your faith everything changes. Your perspective changes, as well as your thoughts.

When my husband died, I never blamed God or asked why. My strong faith consumed me. It moved in ways that I'd never imagined that it could. I had a sense of peace and even joy. You're probably thinking that's just crazy. Well to some it may seem so, but to a believer those thoughts override any doubts. In fact, when bad things happen, and you're a believer something amazing happens. At least this has been my story. My faith becomes my rock; it's unbreakable, strong, and determined. With death comes sadness, of course it does. But when you're a follower of Christ, he gently holds your hand and guides you with his peace and understanding.

There's always a dark side and a bright side. You can either follow the dark side and listen to its negative thoughts, or you can follow the Christ side, which is always the bright positive side. Christ will never guide you into a dark thought or bad situation. He does, however, allow bad things to happen. Those bad things are to build your faith. Without ever having bad things happen your life would be peaceful and tranquil, right? As long as we reside in our human body and reside here on earth that's just never going to be. However, the life after this one will be filled with that and more!

It's interesting how I've always had an intense yearning to write about my faith. For many years that thought sat in the back of my mind, nudging at me and reminding me that I had some unfinished business. Between the everyday duties of operating my manufacturing business and managing a shop, there was little time to contemplate such a grand project. It wasn't until my husband died that this longing became stronger and more intense.

During his four-year battle with cancer, I was blessed and surrounded with peace. Now when I look back, I realize more than ever how God protected me and held me close. There was never any doubt or discouragement about what I wanted to write, after witnessing the miraculous moments that surfaced during his illness and death.

Some people believe that tragedies trigger something in the brain and that when these bad things happen a person turns to God because they can't cope on their own. They believe it's some form of coping mechanism. If you are a born-again Christian you know that this is farthest from the truth.

The miraculous transformation of one that has been born again usually can't describe their new life, because it's not of this world. As humans we require seeing, touching, and hearing to be convinced something is real. That's why some people have a hard time believing in God.

"Then Jesus told him, 'because you have seen me, you have believed; blessed are those who have not seen and yet have believed'."

—JOHN 20:29

It's so hard, you say.

I get it. I'm not going to sugarcoat it and tell you that believing in God is going to be easy, and that your life will be free of burdens and pain. We are human and we make mistakes; we lack trust, patience, understanding, and the list goes on and on. When you are a believer of God, you now have two fathers, and regardless of your relationship with your birth father or adopted father, your heavenly father loves you unconditionally. His constant love is with you always, and he wants you to depend and lean on him for all things both big and small.

Mark

I met Mark over a year ago. He came into my shop one sunny autumn day. That first visit was guided by our faith. Little did I realize how this new friendship was guided by God. Mark became a weekly visitor. We shared our love for the Lord and he would ask if he could pray with me each time he visited. We developed a friendship that was formed with faith. If you've ever experienced this type of friendship then you know that it's perfect in every way. There's an uncommon trust and safety that associates with a friendship of faith.

Through our weekly visits I learned that Mark was a nurse at a nearby hospital. We never really talked about our daily lives because the conversations were always centered on prayer.

I quickly learned later when Lennis's cancer progressed why God sent Mark into my store that sunny fall day.

Lennis had awakened around two-thirty in the morning saying he was having a hard time breathing. I told him that we should go to the hospital and have him checked out. The hospital admitted Lennis and started caring for him. Later that day while sitting in the hospital chair in his room, someone peeked in the door. It was Mark!

I knew through our conversations at the shop that he worked at this hospital but that was about the extent of our conversations. I became curious as to what Mark did at the hospital. I asked him and he explained how he was the assistant director of nursing. A little bell went off in my head at that moment. I realized then that the day Mark visited my shop over a year ago was not an accident. There was a purpose behind it.

Mark continued to visit Lennis throughout his time in the hospital. He would pray over Lennis, and bring comfort and a sense of peace to him that neither myself nor family members could offer. There was one occasion that Lennis got frustrated and filled with anxiety, and I was at a loss as to what to do. I asked the nurse if she could call Mark to visit. Mark arrived within a few minutes. He commented on how the nurse had asked him how he got there so quickly.

He told her how he was on the elevator on the way before he received the call. After Mark prayed over Lennis, I quickly noticed how he calmed down and once again peace surrounded him.

The power that comes with believing and trusting always brings peace no matter what the circumstance.

Today, Mark continues to be an amazing friend and visits my shop. I pray that he will continue on his faithful journey sharing his love for Jesus, and that God will watch over him and keep him safe.

It sometimes seems that the people who come into our lives just happen. I can assure you this is farthest from the truth.

Mark stopped by today to tell me that he was moving back to Virginia Beach. We both marveled at how God brought us together and how our friendship was somehow wrapped with the goodness that God had for both of us. Mark, if you're reading this, you will never know how blessed I am that you came into my life. I'm thankful to God for bringing us together. I miss our talks!

Faith Will Move Mountains

I know you've heard the phrase, *your faith can move mountains*. It seems far-fetched or bizarre to actually believe that your faith could possibly conquer death or despair. When you start reading the Bible you begin to understand just how strong faith really is, and how indeed it can move the tallest of mountains.

If I have the gift of prophecy and can fathom all mysteries and all knowledge, and if I have a faith that can move mountains, but do not have love, I am nothing.

—1 Corinthians 13:2

He replied, "Because you have so little faith. Truly I tell you, if you have faith as small as a mustard seed, you can say to this mountain, 'Move from here to there,' and it will move. Nothing will be impossible for you."

—Matthew 17:20

For it is by grace you have been saved, through faith – and this is not from yourselves, it is the gift of God.

—EPHESIANS 2:8

"Truly I tell you, if anyone says to this mountain, 'Go, throw yourself into the sea,' and does not doubt in their heart but believes that what they say will happen, it will be done for them. Therefore I tell you, whatever you ask for in prayer, believe that you have received it, and it will be yours."

—MARK 11:23-24

Abraham

*F*ive days before Lennis passed I received a phone call from a man named Abraham. He was calling to set up a time to deliver a hospital bed for Lennis.

"Miss Jill," he said, "this is Abraham and I am going to bring Mr. Lennis a bed."

It's funny how when you're caring for a dying person your mind doesn't get too far ahead planning or thinking about the next day. You're in the moment, and your mind kind of stays there.

I had been told that the hospital bed would be set up by the delivery driver, but the old bed would need to be taken down by us. The thought of breaking down the old bed, and moving Lennis out of the bed in his fragile condition was overwhelming to think about while I was caring for him, but those thoughts lasted but only a couple of minutes, and disappeared as quickly as they came.

A sense of peace came over me, and I knew without hesitation that all would be well.

Later that same day I received a text from three brothers that were friends with Lennis. They asked if they could come and visit with Lennis. We arranged a time for them to visit, and while they were visiting I received the call from the delivery driver, Abraham, asking if it was okay to bring the bed.

After telling the three brothers that the bed needed to be broken down in able for the hospital bed to be moved in, they jumped into action like professional movers. In fact, one of the brothers mentioned how he used to work for a moving company. They also helped me move Lennis temporarily into my bed, while the beds were being switched.

After the bed was dismantled and the three brothers left, Abraham came to deliver the hospital bed.

"Hello, Miss Jill, my name is Abraham, and I am going to take care of you and your husband. God is good," he said. His powerful words brought even more peace and I realized at that single moment how blessed I was.

The hospital bed came in pieces, and Abraham began unloading and carrying in the unassembled bed.

We chatted as he carried in a wheelchair, oxygen tanks, and an assortment of other medical paraphernalia, and my home started to take on the appearance of a hospital ward.

All we needed was a walker I thought; no sooner than I had that thought, Abraham appeared carrying one into the house. At the same time I was pondering those thoughts, others flowed through my mind, and I understood that even a hospital bed can be a blessing when someone is dying.

Abraham walked upstairs to the bedroom to set up the bed, and as he walked past the room Lennis was in he said to Lennis, "Hello Mr. Lincoln, I am here to take care of you. Abraham is here, God is good," he said as he walked by my husband's room.

As I listened and watched Abraham I knew what a special soul he was, and my thankful thoughts were sent to God in a little prayer of gratitude.

As Abraham and I visited while he was setting up the hospital bed, I found out that he had come to the United States from Africa some twenty-five years ago.

I offered to help him carry in the heavy pieces of the bed, but he would not allow me to help. I asked him how many beds he delivered during a day and he told me up to twenty-five. He was working diligently to get the bed set up, and to think that he delivered up to twenty-five beds each day blew my mind!

His calm and joyous spirit filled our home, and I loved it when he said, "God is good, Miss Jill," which he repeated every other sentence that he spoke.

I grabbed one of the bed pieces, and Abraham stopped me and said, "No, Miss Jill, that one is *lidafas!*"

"What does that mean?" I asked.

Abraham explained that the word meant *heavy* in his language. We laughed, as I repeated the word, not sounding anything like how he pronounced it.

Abraham got the bed set up and I put clean sheets and pillow cases on it, and then took Lennis under the arm and helped him into the new bed.

After Abraham left, I pondered the events of the day. My mind filled with peace once again, and thankfulness of how the brothers were there to help at just the right time, and how this kind and compassionate man named Abraham seemed like an angel sent from God. *God is good*, I said to myself!

Later that day, as the hospice workers walked up my sidewalk to check on Lennis, I walked outside. My heart was filled with such gratitude from the events of the day that I exclaimed it to the hospice nurse, pastor, and social worker as they were walking towards our home.

"Have you met Abraham?" I asked.

One of them answered, "No, but we've heard many good things about him"

"You need to meet Abraham," I said.

They looked at me with concern as I shared how that day had been filled with blessing after blessing. I didn't care what they thought; I knew how God had worked through the brothers and how he had sent Abraham to calm my soul.

That day was filled with miracles and I will never think otherwise. When you carry your faith with you day-by-day, you're going to see miracles and meet some too! It's not a matter of just trusting, but asking. Asking in trust forms faith!

I later discovered that Abraham was a man who wore many hats. He works as a chauffer on weekends, and is part of a charity organization that helps the people of Gambia by sending second-hand clothing and goods back to his home country. I asked him if it would be okay to share his email with readers of this book and he replied *yes* without hesitation.

If you're wishing to donate to Abraham's charity organization his email is: *abrahamebousarr2018@gmail. com.*

Abraham and I have remained good friends after Lennis' passing, and I'm forever thankful for his friend-ship and kind spirit.

Pat

During the time that Lennis was sick, it was important that I honor his wishes, and not make decisions without his approval. Now that I look back I realize the significance in those thoughts. Honoring someone's dying wishes, especially a loved one's, should not be a choice but a decision. When Lennis told me that he thought it was time to call hospice, my mind tossed back and forth and I realized the severity of the situation that was now at hand.

I awoke the next day with the task of choosing a hospice group. My first thought was *what if I choose one we don't like?* There were lots of second and third thoughts too, but I asked God to direct me on which hospice to choose. I chose five, and waited for them to reply. Within an hour or so almost all had called me back, but there was one that stood out more than the others. It was as though the one that stood out had a beacon shining on it! I knew without any hesitation this was the right one, and set up a time for someone to come to our home. Later that day a nurse named Jenelle called me to set up a visit to evaluate Lennis.

The next day, Jenelle arrived and I escorted her to the guest room where Lennis was. As we were talking she explained how the director of their organization was a local doctor. As soon as she said his name, Lennis and I both looked at one another in awe. The doctor she mentioned had been Lennis' primary care physician and diagnosed his cancer a few years prior. *What were the odds, I thought?*

"Thank you, Jesus!" I said.

The following day, a hospice nurse named Pat called. She told me that she was going to be Lennis' nurse. She arrived mid-afternoon, and as we chatted over the dining room table about last wills, and all of other technical aspects of dying, I could see that this woman was down-to-earth, compassionate and caring. My urge to announce my faith to Pat was overwhelming. As I spoke my truth, Pat explained how she could never be a hospice nurse without her faith and trust in God. I thought about her words as she spoke, and how difficult it must be to travel from home to home caring for dying individuals. I also thought about how thankful that I am for folks like Pat and the work that they do. We are fortunate to have such health options as hospice.

This was all new to me and I knew little about what hospice did except for what I'd heard through the grapevine. Sometimes the grapevine can be misleading and filled with inaccurate information.

I can't say enough good things about them. Although their visits are brief and to-the-point, checking vitals, and monitoring one's health make you feel like you're not dealing with death on your own. Well of course you're not alone! Believe me, God is with you every step of the way!

Nowadays hospice prescribes all of the medications that they feel the patient will need. Typically anxiety meds, morphine, and whatever else is required to help calm the dying person and make their journey a little less painful. They turn over all of the medications over to the caregiver, and teach you how much and when to administer them.

Who knew? I sure didn't! Our guestroom resembled a pharmacy. The little table that was next to the bed was filled with a variety of medications that hospice prescribed. Having the meds readily available offered a sense of peace.

One of the great things about hospice is that when your loved one passes, they send a nurse to officially announce that the person has passed. They clean the body, wrap them in a sheet, and take great care of your loved one. When you visit with the hospice nurse early on, you also discuss choices in funeral homes and arrangements for the body. I found this to be comforting to not have to call a coroner, and wait hours for someone to come.

After the nurse declared that Lennis had passed I peeked in. I found myself not wanting to and wanting to at the same time. I believe these feelings are normal. I can't say that it made me feel any different seeing his body cocooned in the starch white sheet, but it did offer closure.

I often think of Pat the nurse, and how she was always so kind and compassionate. During their first visit they had told me that they would visit every day. When they told me this, I knew Lennis did not have a lot of time left here on earth.

If you have a loved one that is dying, hospice is there to help you, and they do in many ways.

Divine Death

I wrote this chapter much later after finishing this book, but a little voice kept reminding me that it was important to include it.

My mom was a smart soft-spoken woman. She was diagnosed with leukemia after falling and breaking her hip. I'll never forget that icy night driving to her house and seeing her laying in the hallway. She had tried to venture out on the iciest night of the winter and fell on a sheet of black ice, breaking her hip.

The paramedics met me, and I followed the ambulance to the local hospital. I had been sitting with her in the emergency room and went out of the room for just a moment, when I see two doctors walking toward me. They both had that concerned-doctor look on their faces, but I didn't know that it was directed at me.

They told me that my mom had a complication. I remember responding, "Does she need blood?" One of the doctors then told me that my mom had leukemia. I was dazed and confused when I heard this; I could not figure out just how they could have made such a diagnosis. I later found out that leukemia shows up in your blood, and that the blood doesn't lie.

My mom and I had always been close. I valued her strong opinion and advice. She went on to live a fairly normal life and was able to take a chemotherapy pill each day to keep the cancer under control.

Ten years passed, and then she became ill. It was her time and she knew it. She told me that she was ready to leave this world and go to the next. This was not an easy pill for me to swallow, as I would be losing my best friend, but I also knew that God was calling another one of his children to go home.

She asked me one day how I was going to make it without her. If I had answered her question honestly I would have said that I had no idea. But I wanted to protect my mom from my freaked-out feelings, so I replied, "I'll just have to, Mom," with the sternest voice that I could muster up. I wanted her to have peace about leaving this world. I totally faked it! We do this sometimes with a dying person, and we do it to protect them. At least this is what I thought I was doing.

The day that my mom passed was a day like any other, except upon waking up, I knew that she was going to pass that day. I have always felt that God was protecting me. As I got in my car to go to the hospital, emotions were running high—this was just six days after 9-11. I remember telling my mom on that day how she was leaving at a good time because the world was crazy. There again, I felt some form of comfort while saying it with protection wrapped around the thoughts and words. As I entered her hospital room, she lay quietly, as if she were sleeping. I somehow knew that her body was quietly leaving its earthly vessel.

My eyes were glued on her as I watched her weak heartbeat slowing down. After sitting, watching and waiting for that final moment, I remember thinking that I needed some air. However, I wanted to be present when she took her last breath.

As I opened the door to leave, I looked down the hall and my dad was walking towards me. My mom and dad had been divorced for over thirty years, but they had a bond that could not be broken. As my dad entered mom's room, I was in awe, and curious to know how my dad knew to be there. I asked him this same question and he told me that he was getting ready to tee off at the golf course and stopped in his tracks, knowing that he needed to be here!

I was so emotional at the time that I didn't realize this precious gift was from God, and one I would be writing about later. My dad continued sitting on one side of my mom's bed and I on the other. She took her final breath quietly and peacefully. My dad waved to the sky and said, "I love you, Alice," and I in turn waved to the sky and said, "I love you, Mom." The room was quiet and peaceful, and my mom's presence was no longer there.

I wanted to share this story in hopes that you will find solace and faith.

Bittersweet

I often think about when my mother named my company all those years ago. She knew that she was dying when she named my business. After she passed, the name took on a completely different meaning.

During the time that I was taking care of Lennis, I needed to manage my store and maintain the business. Honestly, without faith, there would be no mortal way to handle operating a business daily while caring for a person that needs you.

I'm writing this so that when others encounter the same challenge of needing to make a living while caring for a sick loved one they will be encouraged. Faith becomes even more important when you're juggling a career and being a caregiver at the same time.

When you call upon Jesus during the times that you struggle, he comes through the most it seems during the times that you feel lost and filled with despair.

When I had to tend to the store, I set up a security camera in Lennis's room. My shop is only five minutes from our home. This way if he needed me, I could be home quickly.

Some would think setting a camera in a room in which you're caring for a loved one is odd. My thought is you do what is needed to aid you in any way that you can. The ability to have a camera in his room was a solution to a problem. I could easily check on my husband and monitor his condition while still being able to make a living.

Deborah

*I*t is rare to have the blessing of having a faith-powered friend. Deborah and I met years ago when I was organizing a celebration for our downtown after a tornado ripped through and destroyed many homes and businesses surrounding and on our downtown square.

The event itself was powered by faith, however I didn't recognize it as such until many years later.

It's funny how you remember certain times of your life, the precise moment, place and time when things happen. This is the case for when I first met Deborah. The phone rang and I answered and spoke with this lady named Deborah. We talked for some time on the phone. She was hoping to be a vendor at our downtown event. She ran a health wellness company and was wishing to set up a booth.

We became very good friends after the event. In fact, we spoke on the phone almost every day. Our friendship was built on faith. A friendship built on faith will never disappoint you! I mentioned earlier how a faith friendship is centered on trust and most of all love.

Other friendships that I've had felt different. Not in a bad way but more in a disappointing kind of way. Don't get me wrong, friendships come in many shapes and sizes, and each one is special. A faith friendship does distinguish itself from a non-faith friendship, however.

The week before Lennis passed, my friend Deborah filled in at the shop. When I asked her to fill in for me she did not hesitate. If I could count the number of times that I've asked Deborah to help me, knowing that it's been hundreds of times, not once has she ever been slow to say *yes!*

As we planned the upcoming downtown event, I lay in bed pondering ideas and plans so that it would be a success with our townspeople. The event was a success, and the start of my dear friendship with Deborah.

Peace Be With You

*A*sk yourself, do my thoughts meet God's approval? I can speak personally and say that mine do not. I feel that I'm learning and getting better at pleasing God with my thoughts and actions, but I fall short most of the time. When you become aware of your thoughts you will find that you have the ability under God's grace to make improvements and gradually learn from your mistakes.

Reading the Bible each day helps me to stay grounded and reminds me that I must put on the shield of God's armor each and every day. It's important to ask God for his shield of protection the moment you rise. This helps you to overcome challenges and gives you a full level of protection. Never forget that God has your back. No matter the situation, he's right there with you, no matter how dire the situation.

Not long ago I experienced a negative situation that I wasn't sure how to handle. A person sent me a message via social media that was bitter and filled with evil. This person went on to say horrible and cruel things that were so evil that I couldn't even process them. I knew that I needed to turn the situation over to God.

I asked God to guide me and direct me in my replies to this not-so-nice person. My last and only words to this person were "Peace be with you." As soon as I typed those four words, a peace overcame me, and I was set free.

A few days later that same peace set in and allowed me to realize that this was the only way to respond to such evil and malice. It felt amazing to turn the other cheek! The reason I can say that it felt amazing is because I typically allowed such things to upset me.

Anytime that you have a confrontation with someone like this there is usually nothing you can do or say that will change things. Then I asked myself, *why should I even care what such a person thought of me?* The truth is you shouldn't. God's thoughts about you should be your only concern.

When you are a believer, you are in the world but not of the world. We must train our minds to not react with our thoughts, but to ask Jesus for guidance. *My help comes from the Lord.*

My help comes from the LORD, the Maker of heaven and earth. Indeed, he who watches over Israel will neither slumber nor sleep. the sun will not harm you by day, nor the moon by night. The LORD will watch over your coming and going both now and forevermore.

—PSALM 121

My ability to trust was not always as strong and firm as it is now. Each day as I read the Bible his words became the direction of my life and become a new way of thinking. I have become closer to God through his powerful words.

Good and Evil

*I*t's hard to imagine that we're surrounded by evil. It's more comfortable to believe that we're surrounded by good. There is and always has been good and evil. You may not understand, but the moment you wake it's necessary to put on the shield of God's protection each and every day.

It's also important to read the word of God. I don't mean read the Bible once a week, twice a month. In my life I've found that when I read the Bible every day I build strength in my faith. Honestly, I can tell a huge difference when I don't read the word of God. I'm more anxious, unsettled, and unsure of things. It's easy for negative thoughts to fill my mind. When I read the word on a consistent and daily basis, I feel as though God is by my side protecting me from evil. It's comforting to know that each and every one of us has access to such a valuable teaching book. The Bible is my favorite book!

Recently, I began reading it from the beginning. It's amazing how each time that I read it, different scriptures speak to me in new ways that are different from my past readings. I love that about the Bible!

The truth is that the world that we live in is filled with good and evil. There's a battle going on each moment of each day. When you realize this, you become more aware of it, and can build a defense with the love that God has for you.

I'm not saying that bad things don't happen to me, not at all. In fact, bad things happen all of the time, but there's a change in the way that I react after becoming a follower of Christ. Trying to explain this transformation is one of the hardest things that I've ever done. I'll give it a shot!

My life on earth is surrounded by evil. There's no way of getting around it. It's everywhere! When you are transformed into a true Christian, God gifts you with discernment to recognize evil in a way that you've probably never experienced. You recognize evil for what it is.

How do you deal with it? If you can, walk away, but if you can't, now is a great time to open the Bible. The Bible is filled with stories about evil. In fact most of it was written about evil. There has always been evil in our world, and we've always been surrounded by it. There really isn't any difference in evil of today compared to evil of yesterday. Evil is evil! The key and most important thing is that you see it for what it is, and know how do deal with it.

Do you fight evil with evil? When someone hurts you or gossips about someone else, do you join in or do you walk away? All the years of joining in seem to have been such a waste of time. I'll blame it on my Scottish blood! When I became a born-again, walking away or not joining in offered a sense of not only peace, but fulfillment and joy.

I mentioned how I was a part of the evil team, often joining in with a gossipy co-worker or person. When I became a born-again, it became clear how trivial and silly and downright unacceptable this old behavior was. When you become a part of the gossip, you take away the peace that you have with God. Who cares if you're not of that crowd! I would rather be able to shout to the mountains that I'm not a follower of evil, but a follower of Christ. I can assure you, the latter is by far the most rewarding. I know, I've lived both ways!

The Reward

*Y*ou may ask yourself why I believe in God and the Bible. It's easy to say that you believe in something, and not follow through with those beliefs. When you follow Christ and begin reading the Bible every day, you become closer to God. You see how the stories of the Bible are so relevant to today. In fact, the words of the Bible touch my heart in ways that cannot be touched.

The Bible teaches us that when we turn our heart over to God and ask him into our lives that our reward is everlasting life. In other words, when I ask God to forgive me of my sins, and make Jesus my Lord and Savior, I'm also asking for forgiveness. With those simple but sincere thoughts and words comes the gift of everlasting life.

Let me ask you, who doesn't want to live forever? I can't even imagine everlasting life in the kingdom of heaven. Well, that's not true, I can imagine, but I know my imagination falls short of the glorious heaven that exists!

When I was born again, the significance of Jesus dying on the cross overwhelmed me, and it always made me cry. Jesus was the only human who never sinned. This makes sense only because Jesus is God's son. When he was nailed to the cross he was fighting for you, the sinner. His final words, "It is finished," explain that.

From that moment in the garden with Adam and Eve until this moment, humans have been filled with sin. Our God is an all-knowing God. He knows what's going to happen before it happens. He knows your future before you know it. He knows what decisions you'll make before you make them. He knows the names of each and every star. He knows how many hairs are on your head. He knows everything! Just imagine this for a moment. It's a lot to take in.

"Truly, truly, I say to you, he who hears my word, and believes Him who sent me, has eternal life, and does not come into judgment, but has passed out of death into life."

—JOHN 5:24

"For God so loved the world that He gave His only begotten Son, that whoever believes in Him shall not perish, but have eternal life."

—JOHN 3:16

Being a Christian isn't easy. We live in a world filled with evil, mistrust, jealousy, and the list goes on and on. I'm often reminded how being a Christian means *being a Christian*. Forgiving others and doing things that I believe would be pleasing to God. What is pleasing to God? Giving the sacrifice God wants.

"Therefore by Him let us continually offer the sacrifice of praise to God, that is, the fruit of our lips, giving thanks to His name. But do not forget to do good and to share, for with such sacrifices God is well pleased."

—HEBREWS 13:15-16

Good Works and Faith

*W*hen I began reading scripture about good works, I was taken to James 2:14:

What good is it, my brothers and sisters, if someone claims to have faith but has no deeds? Can such faith save them?

—JAMES 2:14

The question is can you have one without the other? The answer is no. Of course God wants each of us to help our neighbors and give to others, but if you give without faith, you're not really giving. A lot of times we give to make ourselves feel better.

Jesus, the son of God lived his life giving to the poor and healing the sick. He, of course, was the son of God so his faith was grounded by his love for his father. He knew what pleased his father, and he without failing dedicated and lived his life as his father wished.

Think about that for a moment. The son of God, knowing he was the son of God. He also knew his future. When you read Mark 8:31 you can see that Jesus predicted his death.

He then began to teach them that the Son of Man must suffer many things and be rejected by the elders, the chief priests and the teachers of the law, and that he must be killed and after three days rise again.

—MARK 8:31

This is a lot to take in, and I find that it's necessary to read this passage more than once. First comes faith, and then comes good works. It sounds simple enough, doesn't it?

You know that feeling of giving that seems to be blanketed with God's love? It's not a feeling of gratifying yourself, but only to give from a heart filled with the love for Jesus.

In other words, you're not giving for you, but you're giving because God is directing you to give. You'll know it when God is directing you to give, and you will begin to recognize his loving guidance.

Judgment

There isn't enough paper for me to write down the number of times someone has offended me or treated me with malice. Before I became a born-again Christian, I would describe myself as a rebel. I'd quickly lash back, and get angry. I always blamed this behavior on my Scottish blood. No offense Scottish ancestors!

Once I began to read the Bible more and take in the scripture, it became clear that my behavior was only hurting me. Most importantly, my anger and judgment took me further away from my faith. These feelings didn't just disappear overnight. It has been a process of turning to God and praying diligently.

Do you remember when I mentioned earlier how we are surrounded by evil every day? It's important that you remember this, because it helps you to remain strong in your faith, which is your shield against evil. There are many scriptures about this, and in fact the entire Bible is filled with numerous readings referencing good and evil.

I'm also not trying to make light of how hard it is to turn the other cheek. Of course, there are instances when it's best to simply walk away. I've come to learn through many years of living that God's teachings are always the best way to live your life.

You see, that's it! We are all guilty of judging each other and also putting others in the box that we think they should be in. I'm guilty of this as are you. We are human, and it's impossible to not have these types of feelings occasionally.

What I've learned is that when I read the word of God I become more aware of this human fault and start to correct my thinking to a non-judgmental view. After all, we're all different, we don't think the same. Our views may even be opposite, but the idea of trusting in God and studying his teachings offers a better understanding of how transforming your life to becoming not so judgmental starts to grow and is cultivated through your faith.

Judge not, that ye be not judged. For with what judgment ye judge, ye shall be judged: and with what measure ye mete, it shall be measured to you again. And why beholdest thou the mote that is in thy brother's eye, but consider not the beam that is in thine own eye?

—MATTHEW 7:1-3 (KJV)

Over the years and through my life I have been guilty of judging others. In reality, it's impossible for a human to not judge another human. So often I have judged only to be wrong about my judgments, but I didn't seem to learn from my judgmental mistakes, because it seemed I repeated them over and over.

It wasn't until my husband became ill and I became a caregiver that I was more aware of our judgmental world and how I fell prey into its trap. After he passed, I had a keen eye for judgmental comments and quickly became aware of just how judgmental our world is.

The Internet has added glory to the judgment realm. It seems that everyone has a viewpoint, and if you aren't in agreement with their point of view, you are wrong. Think about that last sentence for a moment. Someone shares their opinion, and you don't agree, so you begin the dreaded social media debate, and next thing you know you've spent hours thrashing out your different views.

Now think about that sentence. You've spent hours trying to convince the other person or persons that your argument is valid and that they are wrong in their method of thinking. I don't know about you, but for me this is not how I desire to spend my time. You will find that nothing gets resolved and the person that you are debating is not going to change how they think. Now once again, think about that sentence. We are trapped and we can't get out!

I often ponder how many hours I've spent doing this only to be disappointed in myself for falling into the trap. Whether it's political views or just plain life views, it's easy to learn what other's point of views are even if you're not interested in them at all. Judgment accompanies these debates and it quickly becomes a vicious circle of mistrust and confusion.

Inside Out and Upside Down

S ometimes only a few words are needed to describe what happens when you ask Jesus into your life. Putting it simply and to the point: when you are transformed into a follower of Christ, he turns you inside out and upside down. Once you turn your heart over to God, your attitude changes and you have a skip in your walk, situations that once hindered you now teach you and draw you closer to God.

Think about it for a moment. If you lived your life without any challenges it would be difficult to appreciate the good! If it were all good, then good would look the same. But when you have bad things happen, you really appreciate the good. Not only do bad events, loss, death, malice, etc. happen to you as a follower of Christ, these difficult life moments strengthen your faith.

This is what God wants. He doesn't want bad things to happen to you, but he knows that bad things will happen.

I've heard folks ask when something bad happens, "Why did God let this happen?" The truth is I do not know the answer to this question, but God does.

If you start believing that God has the answer and trust in his timing, I guarantee one thing, in the end it will make sense and good will come from it.

All things work together for good to them that love God and are called according to his purpose.

—ROMANS 8:28

Luke 7

*T*he other night I was awakened in the middle of the night, and God directed me to a scripture in the Bible, in particular Luke 7.

As I began to read Luke 7, I had to read it several times to understand the meaning. I encourage you to read this chapter of the Bible. You may need to read it several times like I did, to understand the message that God is trying to convey. In fact, there is more than one message, but all are significant teachings from God that stand strong and true today.

Jesus said to the woman, "Your faith has saved you; go in peace."

—LUKE 7:50

This chapter in Luke is filled with many wonders!

All people are created equal. A poor woman is just as important to the Lord as a rich one. There's only one thing that God cares about and that is your faith and trust in him. Nothing else matters. Just as your birth father or adopted father loves you unconditionally, your heavenly father loves you in the same way. The difference is that his love is supernatural. We can't understand the breadth or intensity of God's love for us, because we're human. The Creator of all things loves you and will not forsake you no matter what.

And I pray that you, being rooted and established in love, may have power together with all of the Lord's holy people, to grasp how wide and long and high and deep is the love of Christ, and to know this love that surpasses knowledge – that you may be filled to the measure of all the fullness of God.

—EPHESIANS 3:18-19

This is how trust is built. Brick by brick, stone by stone, your faith grows each day as you turn to him for all things in life. The best way I have found to turn to him is by reading his word.

Remind the people to be subject to rulers and authorities, to be obedient, to be ready to do whatever is good, to slander no one, to be peaceable and considerate, and always to be gentle toward everyone.

—TITUS 3:10

At one time we too were foolish, disobedient, deceived and enslaved by all kinds of passions and pleasures. We lived in malice and envy, being hated and hating one another. But when the kindness and love of God our Savior appeared, he saved us, not because of righteous things we had done, but because of his mercy. He saved us through the washing of rebirth and renewal by the Holy Spirit, whom he poured out on us generously through Jesus Christ our Savior. So that, having been justified by his grace, we might become heirs having the hope of eternal life.

—TITUS 3:3-7 (NIV)

When I read the word of God, it's necessary for me to read scripture over and over. It's interesting how when you read the Bible you interpret a different meaning each time that you read it. Depending on when you read it, how you read it, and where you are in life, the words will more than likely resonate differently each time. This is a beautiful thing! This is why the Bible is such a valuable life tool.

Soulful Reading

*D*o you ever recall someone asking you *if you lived on a deserted island and could only take one thing, what would it be?* Have you ever heard anyone answer that they'd want the Bible? I believe it safe to say, probably not. Most people's minds travel to must-have survival tools, like water and food. The Bible would more than likely be the last thing that you would think to have. To say the significance of its pages would be lifesaving would seem to be over the top and out there!

Just as exercise and eating well are part of a healthy lifestyle, so too is reading the Holy Bible. We set goals for weight loss, and are determined to change our diets, but we usually underestimate the importance of reading the word.

Sometimes when I'm busy and preoccupied with business and life, I find myself skipping my Bible reading, only to realize that when this happens my soul feels incomplete and uneasy. Some of you may be familiar with this feeling.

Because we are human and live in a sinful world filled with darkness and evil, it is important to put the shield of God on each and every day. This shield of protection feeds your soul with God's love.

The Bible is our shield, and as we read it, we are reminded of God's unconditional love and how he is always with us wherever we go. You may say to yourself, *I don't need to read the Bible, I believe in God, and that he is with me.* It is easy to believe this, but my heart knows that when I open that book and begin to read the powerful words within its pages, there's a difference between just believing and following his teachings. I get a sense of well-being and wholeness that cannot be duplicated in any other earthly experience.

Not too long ago, I heard a preacher tell his congregation that if it's been awhile since you read the Bible, start with the book of Psalms and read one each day. Psalms are powerful teachings that are easy to read. They are also encouraging words that will guide you through everyday life.

The Perfect Place

*I*f you're a believer in Christ then you probably also believe that he guides you and directs your path. It's not an accident that you are where you are. Sometimes our directions are shifted, but believe me, God knows exactly where you should be at any given time. *Isn't that amazing?*

It's certainly a challenge to believe that God has the ability to guide each believer in the direction that they are meant to go in, isn't it? He is an all-knowing God. He has the supernatural ability to know everything and to know what you're going to do before you do it. It's hard to wrap your head around it, but as you acquaint yourself with the Bible and its teachings, you will begin to understand this to be true.

It's also difficult to imagine a God that is perfect. I've never met anyone who I'd consider to be perfect, so there is no gauge for comparison. It's taken me awhile to understand and realize that God's perfect love *is* perfect. None of us are capable of understanding just what perfect is. We are human, God is not. We are all surrounded by God's perfect love, and the more that we study his word and pray and give him our hearts, we also begin to understand. I can't tell you exactly how this works, but I can assure you that it you will feel peace and happiness that you've never experienced.

When I first opened my shop those many years ago, I knew that the location I chose was the one that God wanted for me. In fact, I never once doubted this. There is a certain supernatural peace that comes when one has discernment from God. Believing that you are where you are supposed to be and doing what you're supposed to be doing is a gift. If your purpose has yet to be revealed, I promise you that through prayer, it will be. I always find myself going back to that word. *Prayer!*

Rejoice always, pray without ceasing, give thanks in all circumstances; for this is the will of God in Christ Jesus for you.
                                           —1 THESSALONIANS 5:16-18

Have I not commanded you? Be strong and courageous.

                                           —JOSHUA 1:9

I'm a firm believer in God's timing. It's taken years to

realize that my time is not God's time. How often have I become impatient or discouraged because the results that I expected or imagined didn't create the results that I'd planned. Sometimes years later, the plan seems as though it was perfectly designed and exceeded my expectations.

This has happened over and over in my life, and has allowed me to realize that my plan is somewhat pointless, but that God's plan is perfect. I can't count the number of times I've depended on my plans, only to see them crumble. But when I pray for guidance and direction and read the Holy Bible, those plans always exceed my wildest dreams! I'm seeing a pattern. This is a pattern designed by God—perfect in every way, filled with his perfect love.

In Leviticus 11:44 and 1 Peter 1:16 we read *"Be holy as I am holy."* Many have understood this to mean that we are required to be perfect, like God. If we could be perfect on our own or simply encouraged to be, we wouldn't need the sacrifice of Jesus.

In the New Testament, the word for holy is *"hagios"* and means *set apart, reverent, sacred*, and *worthy of veneration*. This word applies to God, because God Himself is totally other, separate, sacred, transcendent, reverent, and set apart from every created thing. The Third Person of the Trinity is called the Holy Spirit. He too is fully God, and all three Persons of the Trinity are holy and have the weight of glory abounding in them.

Glory to God

*A*fter my husband passed, there was a question that I heard over and over from friends. *How are you doing? Are you doing okay? I bet that you are sad.* It wasn't difficult to answer, but the answer was surprising to most. In fact, obviously there was a void and I missed my husband, but I also knew that a few months before he passed he confessed his faith in Jesus and asked him to come into his heart.

I realized that these questions were asked with sincerity, concern, and love, but I also realized that my feelings were not what most people experience after the death of a loved one. I had an overwhelming peace that exceeded sadness or despair. Knowing that my husband had a new life in heaven and one that would last forever offered this peace.

This was when I decided to write this book. Those two questions made me realize how important it is to have faith and understand the unconditional love and forgiveness that my Father has for me. My husband's death was a breezeway to want to learn more and have a better understanding of God's teachings.

If you stop and think about our earthly lifespan, it seems to be a lengthy period of time. However, if you become a believer in Christ and follow his guidance, your life after death is eternal. I think about that world a lot. *How long is eternal? How long is forever?* No matter how much time I spend pondering these thoughts, my mind can never imagine just how long that is!

I can safely say however that forever is filled with glory and magnificence! Can you imagine being in the same space as Jesus and God? Honestly, I can't, but I do know how spectacular it will be!

So when folks asked me how I was doing and I replied that I was doing fine, their expression was disbelief. I began to realize that maybe some people didn't believe in everlasting life, or possibly they never stopped to think about it. I felt alone, but not in the way of being lonely. I felt alone simply because I felt that my feelings were isolated. *Was I the only one that felt like this after a loved one passed?* I couldn't imagine that I was.

Each day came and each day that same question was asked. *Are you okay?* "I am doing well," I would answer. The look in their eyes was always the same as they had the same look of disbelief and doubt. Then I began to realize that my faith was what formed my strong sense of peace and even happiness.

You're asking yourself, *how can you answer that question saying that you're happy?* One would imagine that would be the last feeling you'd have after a loved one has passed. You'd question the person's integrity and judgment.

Though you have not seen him, you love him; and even though you do not see him now, you believe in him and are filled with an inexpressible and glorious joy, for you are receiving the end result of your faith, the salvation of your souls.

—1 PETER 1:8

Hope

We've all had hope for something. Hope for a better world, hope for peace, and the list goes on and on. It's difficult to have faith without hope and vice versa. But without hope, your faith will not withstand the test of time.

How many times have you been in a situation where it seems that all hope has been lost? It's easy to lose hope, but through faith you gain an understanding that there is always hope. You never lose sight of that through your faith.

As it is written: "I have made you a father of many nations." He is our father in the sight of God, in whom he believed— the God who gives life to the dead and calls into being things that were not.

—ROMANS 4:17,19

Against all hope, Abraham in hope believed and so became the father of many nations, just as it had been said to him. "So shall your offspring be." Without weakening his faith, he faced the fact that his body was as good as dead—since he was about one-hundred year's old—and that Sarah's womb was also dead. Yet he did not waver through unbelief regarding the promise of God, but was strengthened in his faith and gave glory to God, being fully persuaded that God had power to do what he promised.

—ROMANS 4:18-25

The angel of the Lord came and sat down under the oak in Ophrah that belonged to Joash the Abiezrite, where his son Gideon was threshing wheat in a winepress to keep it from Mideanites. When the angel of the Lord appeared to Gideon, he said, "The Lord is with you, mighty warrior." "Pardon me, my lord," Gideon replied, "but if the Lord is with us, why has all this happened to us? Where are all his wonders that our ancestors told us about when they said, did not the Lord bring us up out of Egypt?" But now the Lord has abandoned us and given us into the hand of Midian. The Lord turned to him and said, "Go in the strength you have and save Israel out of Midian's hand. Am I not sending you?"

—JUDGES 6:11, 13-14

My Faith, Your Faith

*A*non-believer is as important to God as a believer. My faith is strong, but that doesn't mean that I'm superior to a non-believer.

It's not easy being a Christian, and in fact I'm not going to tell you that it is. It's downright challenging most of the time. I'm in constant check with my emotions and feelings. Having said that—being a believer in Christ is unlike anything I've ever encountered.

Think about giving birth to your first child or marrying the love of your life, both events are nothing short of amazing, but as I become closer to God, I realize that these life events were a gift from God and that my relationship with him far exceeds even life's best moments. I haven't always thought that way, but when I became stronger in my faith and consistent in reading the Bible my feelings changed.

Our defense for someone who slanders or treats us with malice is Christ. My favorite words are *peace be with you!* I try to remind myself of those words frequently. You will find that when you respond with these words, grace fills your heart and you have peace within you. This is not an accident, this is God's grace and love for you.

The Authority of the Bible

*Y*ou may be asking yourself why there is so much emphasis on reading the Bible. The truth is, and I'm going to put it bluntly, until you accept the authority of the Bible, you will not defer to it. Like a hiker in the woods that has lost his or her way without a compass, they don't know which way to go next. This was a revelation to me!

What I noticed was that every time I read the Bible, my heart was filled with joy compared to the days that I did not read it. The days that I read its words, no matter what the context, there was a difference in the way that I felt, a feeling of being whole and safe. I was not aware of these feelings for many years. Those moments when I began meditating on God's word and reading the Bible were the moments that transformed my life.

The Bible and its contents are filled with powerful teachings that help me to become a better human. The great thing about understanding the words within it and using those words as your guide are a beautiful gift.

As newborn babes, long for the guileless milk of the word in order that by it you may grow unto salvation.

—1 Peter 2:2

Your words were found and I ate them, and Your word became to me the gladness and joy of my heart.

—Jeremiah 15:16

That He might sanctify her, cleansing her by the washing of the water in the word.

—Ephesians 5:26

We may understand that we need the washing of our sins by the Lord's blood, but we also need to realize that we need the washing away of our natural life by His life. *How do we get this washing of life?* The washing water of life is in God's Word. So even if we don't remember or fully understand what we read, our daily Bible reading still washes us from so many negative things.

Are we to believe the Bible when those words run contrary to contemporary culture? We sometimes find in the Bible what we want to find in the Bible. Sometimes we don't understand the Bible. We often misinterpret the Bible. There are words in the Bible that are plain and clear, and there are pages that are hard to understand.

There's no wrong way to read the Bible. As you begin to start reading it everyday, you will notice that you develop a better understanding of God's words. You will also notice a transformation in your way of thinking.

I encourage you to continue reading as it is God's perfect truth and a gift is in his words. You will begin to notice as you read the Bible that it makes more sense, and you'll begin to realize what an impact it has on your life.

Precious Jewels

We often think about our personal belongings as objects of desire. We have a favorite this or that. If you have children or grandchildren, you quickly learn what's really important. Children teach the importance of having human-to-human relationships and most of the time they could care less about what kind of clothes mom wears or how big her diamond ring is. In reality, children teach us a valuable lesson: They remind us of how precious a gift our time and teachings are.

When I was a little girl, I used to love visiting my grandmother Lola. She lived in a tiny house with sweet peas climbing up the side of it. There was a tiny creek with crawdads in her front yard. Every spring we would find mushrooms in her yard. Her easel and sewing kit were neatly sitting in the corner of her bedroom, as if she would be ready to replace a button or paint a picture at any moment.

My memories are always centered on overnight stays and bedtime stories. Those special moments spent with my grandmother will forever touch me in ways that can never be duplicated.

Grandma's Bible was always in the same spot, tucked inside a shelf on a cabinet in her bedroom. As I lay in her bed, I could see the worn Bible, and thought about how often she read from it. Often I would ask her about it and she'd grab it from the shelf and read it to me. Her kind and gentle nature were consistent and she shared her love freely and generously.

In fact, I know that my grandmother read her Bible everyday. She read it to her granddaughter, who was too young to understand the words. But those words stuck as I grew to be a young woman, and as I write this book they stick to every page.

This is what I refer to as seeds, but not just any seeds, these seeds are unlike any other. These seeds grow to withstand storms and become strong and unwavering. Each of us is a teacher when it comes to spreading the love of God. Someone once told me that the first person to greet you in heaven will be the first person that shared the Bible with you. My grandmother Lola will meet me at the golden gates of heaven.

Mourning
Has Broken

When my husband died, I was sad, but comforted by knowing that he was going to have eternal life. So my sadness was also wrapped in joy.

The truth is, we each experience death differently. What I have learned is that not all grief is created equal. When you love someone for almost thirty years, and they die, sadness comes—however, when you call upon Christ, that sadness transforms into peace.

When I lost my mom, sadness overcame me, as we were best friends, but I also felt that it was necessary to move on. She once asked me how I was going to make it without her. When I answered her with *I will just have to*, my heart knew that it was going to be one of the most difficult things I'd ever done. I didn't want to burden my mom with feelings of guilt as she was dying. Hours after she died, I cried for hours non-stop. Then after I couldn't cry anymore, I realized that life does go on, and I had to live my life without her.

There was a difference between my mom's passing and my husband's death. I wasn't a born-again believer when my mom passed, but I was when my husband died. At the time that my mom died, I knew no difference in how you feel when you're a believer in Christ. Once I shared my heart with God, those feelings of grief changed dramatically. I realized this dramatic difference in my feelings after Lennis passed.

You see, I'd never really thought how grief accumulates differently in each loss. The word *accumulate* best describes grief. Your feelings go back and forth, up and down, they grow, and then they slowly fade into shadows. I don't believe that they ever completely go away. I never imagined learning about myself through loss, but I did.

After Lennis died, there was an tangible sense of peace that surrounded me. As the days passed, I began to notice how each day brought with it different emotions, but sadness no longer accompanied my feelings. My life changed overnight, but my faith remained strong and gave me strength in ways that I never imagined.

Now months later, I realize each day after his death was directed by God, as I prayed and asked for guidance each day. The knowledge of knowing that he asked Jesus into his heart before he passed offered peace within me, and even though challenges crossed my path, like they often do in life, that peace never left. It remained strong and unwavering.

I'm not going to tell you that you won't miss your loved one, but I can safely say that if you're a believer, he will comfort you and give you the gift of peace, not just when you're facing death, but each and every day.

Death is a part of life. The truth is that we all grieve differently. There is no wrong way to grieve. The difference in my grief was, and is, that I'm a believer. The difference in my grief is that, even though I miss my husband, my heart is filled with peace.

It's hard to put into words the difference in how one feels when you believe, but there is a miraculous transformation. I wouldn't know this had I not experienced the death of a loved one before I was born again and then after. I'm sharing this with you for that reason and that reason only, hoping and praying that you too will accept this gift from God. *My strength is made perfect in weakness.*

Worry Not

*D*o not worry. Why do you worry? If you are a Christian, do you worry? I can't speak for anyone but myself and tell you that worry is upon me, but through faith I worry not. It's a process to receive this gift. As I've grown older, it is clear that worry has not been my friend. I've learned that worry brings no change, and with worry comes grief. Both are emotions that we can learn to overcome through faith. God will help you along the way, so don't worry!

Then Jesus said to his disciples: "Therefore I tell you, do not worry about your life, what you will eat; or about your body, what you will wear. For life is more than food, and the body more than clothes. Consider the ravens; they do not sow or reap, they have no storeroom or barn; yet God feeds them. And how much more valuable you are than birds! Who of you by worrying can add a single hour to your life?"

—LUKE 12:22-26

When You Say
You're A Christian

*O*f all the things that I am or hope to become the most important is that I lead by example. How often have you met someone and they have told you that they're a Christian only to contradict everything that you believe a Christian should be.

If you read the Bible then you know that the disciples were far from perfect. Yet Jesus chose these imperfect men to teach his word to the world. Have you ever wondered why? Paul and Matthew, Peter, and the other disciples were God's spokespersons. They felt God's love within their hearts and were compelled to share his message and love with not just certain people, but with everyone.

Anything that causes mistrust or confusion is not of God. He has graciously given you a free will to decide and choose for yourself how you wish to either play along or take the road less traveled. The Internet is filled with opportunities of good, but it is also filled with evil. Just as in all of life one must ask for discernment to recognize the difference.

Sometimes when I pray for discernment, I find that God waits and allows me to learn things the hard way. He knows exactly which path I'm going to take and always guides me when I'm lost. If you ask him to come into your life he will do the same for you. His children are his most precious gift.

"I am the truth, the way, and the life."

—JOHN 14:6

When Words
Are Empty

*H*ow often have you said something only to find out later that you could have said it in a different, more kind and compassionate way? Honestly, not only am I guilty of this, but it's evident in others as well. The truth is our words can sometimes be empty.

I'm learning to think about my words before I speak, and putting a sincere effort into how my words can affect the other person. Once you start the process of minding what you speak, you'll notice how your words are no longer empty but filled with understanding and empathy. We all yearn for this unity, but seldom stop and think about how the words that we use can be filled with love or, conversely, even jealousy and mistrust. I can assure you this, everyone is going through something challenging, and your words cannot only offer comfort, but love.

Kind words provide many benefits. Not only to the person they are intended for, but also to the person who is saying them.

Kind words are like honey, sweet to the soul and healthy for the body.

—PROVERBS 16:24

The thoughts of the wicked are an abomination to the LORD; but the words of the pure are pleasant words.

—PROVERBS 15:26

Gentle words are a tree of life; a deceitful tongue crushes the spirit.

—PROVERBS 15:4

Since God chose you to be the holy people he loves, you must clothe yourselves with tenderhearted mercy, kindness, humility, gentleness, and patience.

—COLOSSIANS 3:12

The last verse is my favorite. One of the tools that we have to help keep our words kind and gentle is reading God's word. The Bible is stuffed full of valuable scripture that aids us in understanding the importance of our words, and how crucial they are to building a relationship with both your heavenly Father and his Son. The Bible is a guidebook that I can't live without. Its contents are powerful teachings that not only encourage me day-by-day, but also guide me.

There's a lot that we don't know about God, but the Bible tells us that his eternal power and divine nature are continually being revealed throughout the earth even to those who have never read the Bible. So how is it that some people fail to see it?

The heavens declare the glory of God; the skies proclaim the work of his hands. Day after day they pour forth speech; night after night they reveal knowledge.

—PSALMS 19:1-2

Please continue to read Psalms 19 as it will help you to understand the living word of God.

If you're new to reading the Bible, Psalms is a wonderful way to expand your knowledge of God's teachings. As you read through Psalms you will have a better understanding of living out his word.

Learning from Other Christians

I am always astounded by how much other Christians and fellow believers teach me. A brief moment is all it takes to help me to better understand how God works his miraculous ways through his followers.

I met Brenda, her husband and son, Ben, a few years ago at my shop. This family stood out as believers, and as we got to know one another I realized their faith and belief in God had captured my attention. During their visits to the shop we always had lengthy conversations about God.

Brenda told me one day how she and her family prayed before leaving their home. They always asked God for guidance and discernment and protection. As Brenda was explaining her family's prayer moments, a *light bulb moment* occurred. I realized how significant and crucial prayer is for our daily life. It caused me to realize even more how prayer is one of our secret weapons against evil, and by praying we form a shield of protection that cannot be penetrated. Our faith in prayer should be strong and unwavering. We should honor our prayer time and give God glory each and every day.

This family has reaffirmed my belief in how God's people spread sunshine and love, and every believer teaches truths through their works. We each have a purpose and sometimes the direction we need can be found by another Christian. Sometimes we learn from non-believers too. There are differences in what we learn from both.

You Be You

*I*t's easy to get wrapped up with image and appearance as we're bombarded with social media platforms that lead us to believe we're not functioning at our full potential. First let me say, your potential has no boundaries in God's eyes. He doesn't care if you've written books, worked your way up to manager or been featured on television. Society cares, but God doesn't. When you begin focusing on your faith and building trust between you and God, you soon begin to realize that this is what's important, and your life will be designed around Him.

Before I became a born-again Christian my world seemed filled with superficial feelings. I always felt fortunate to have the many opportunities that came my way through my business, but it always felt like something was missing. Little did I know the missing link was God. If I hadn't experienced a before and after I wouldn't be able to recognize the supernatural effects of the after.

Having national television coverage, being a radio show host, and appearances on numerous local news segments over the years sound like a small business owner's success story. In reality, each one of those things felt as though I was climbing a ladder to success, but as wonderful as it sounds, it always felt as though something was missing. I could never put my finger on what that something was until I became a born-again Christian.

The moment I turned my heart over to God, my life transformed and I began learning how my faith and love for Christ brought euphoric feelings that I'd never experienced because of any television appearance or magazine article. I know that they are a part of my story and significant, but they are not the happy ending to the story. The happy ending is and always will be wrapped in faith and trust in God.

A Purpose to Live

I recently read a survey conducted by Arizona Christian University that three-quarters of millennials said they are struggling to find direction in life. The study went on to say that while 22% of millennials contend that life is sacred, half of the generation (50 percent) assert that "life is what you make it; there is no absolute value associated with human life."

As I was reading this it made me sad, but it also helped me to realize how as humans we are in need of guidance and direction. This realization also comes with warnings. Being true to yourself and God at the same time is impossible. Unless you're true to God first and yourself second. If you practice this thought, and it does take practice, you will notice a tremendous improvement in your life's purpose.

Throughout my life I've always felt that I had a purpose, but knew that my idea of purpose wasn't always designed by God. Once I began to call upon the Lord for guidance and discernment, my life was filled with an abundance of what I like to call *heavenly purpose*. This new profound purpose is flawless and perfect in the way that only God can produce. When you pray and ask God to give you purpose I promise he won't let you down. In fact, you will be astounded and amazed just how he will work to help you learn your purpose.

Not in a million years or in my wildest dreams would I ever imagine my purpose was to be a soap maker and apothecary shop owner. Some might think that it's necessary to have a business plan for your business to be successful or climb to the next level. I'm not saying that's a bad idea. However, I am saying that it's not necessary when you place your trust in God.

I look back on the days when my soap company was just starting. The lessons and ups and downs were a constant daily occurrence, and there were countless times when I just wanted to give up. Every time that I prayed and asked for guidance from God something would happen.

One time after closing my shop for the day, I had considered shutting everything down. This was during the housing crisis and the economy was looking bleak. I was on the phone with the telephone company to cancel my service when another call came through. It was a customer wanting to place an order.

Knowing that I had prayed over my decisions and not knowing whether those decisions were set in stone allowed me to know that the order was a sign. I recall even saying out loud, *"I get it!"* to God. That was the only time I've ever felt unsure about what I was doing, but that didn't detour me from asking God for guidance, not just in bad times but the good too.

In fact, once I began to learn how God designed my purpose, there was never a question about whether I should be doing what I was doing. As I began meeting people through my business, it became clear this was my purpose. Even as insignificant as it seemed, God had a purpose for it all. Most people would attribute this to luck. Having had both luck and divine direction, I happily say to you—there is a huge difference.

My Bible

Some time ago I had a friend whose daughter went to the same small town church that I attended when I was young. One night I had a dream in which I saw my Bible sitting on a shelf with other Bibles in the basement of the church. The dream seemed more like a vision, but I was asleep.

The next morning I was eager to ask my friend's daughter if she would look to see if indeed my Bible was on the shelf when she attended church on Sunday. I remember getting the Bible when I was around ten or so. My name was engraved on the binding, so I knew that there would be no doubt when found that it was my Bible from all those years ago.

A few days passed and I received a call from my friend's daughter. She told me that my Bible was sitting on the shelf in the basement just as I had told her that it was. She asked a lady at the church if she could give it to me, and the lady agreed. I couldn't believe after all those years that I'd recovered the precious book. I also was amazed about the dream that I'd had and how I knew without a doubt that my Bible was sitting on that shelf.

The old Bible is worn and tattered and has been bound together with tape. It's been borrowed, buried, and bestowed, and now it is home with its owner. I have thought about this dream and vision a lot over the years. I was ten years old when the Bible was dedicated to me. It's nothing short of a miracle that I had such a dream.

Do you believe in visions from God? As a child it seemed that these types of premonitions were common and as I grew to an adult they still happened, but not as frequent. I can't help but believe that these experiences are treasured gifts from God. Whenever I have visions or dreams, I'm reminded of God's love for me. Just like the dream about owning a shop, the Bible dream was also a special gift and I will tuck it away for safe keeping. Whenever I want to be reminded, I'll read this chapter!

It's good to be reminded. When you take time from your busy day to read God's word, you are reminded of not only his love, but his devotion. Yes, God is *devoted* to his followers. He is a proud father when you read the Bible and chat about him with your friends. It's a joy for me to share my stories with others to remind them of his forever love.

Morning Walks

*A*bout ten years ago I started taking two-mile walks in my neighborhood. It wasn't intentional or planned to make this quiet, fresh-air time a spiritual time, but that is what it's turned into. Ten years later and my morning walks are the highlight of my day. There are unique stories that I've gathered through these walks— some of which I share, and some I hold close to my heart.

My walking route hasn't changed much over the years, in fact Elle and I, my cairn terrier have walked past the same houses everyday for ten years. During those years I've witnessed folks selling their homes and new families moving in. New puppies are getting accustomed to their new homes, and young humans are getting older. I'm amazed at how much I learn about my neighbors by simply walking by their homes each day!

As I walk past other people walking, sometimes they say "*hi*," while other times they bow their heads—a method of acknowledgment without talking to let me know that they do not wish to be disturbed. Each person is in their own world, while I am in mine. Sometimes we interact, while other times we don't. In the summer, I see neighbors chatting with neighbors, and as I walk by they say "*hi*," and sometimes we carry on about the weather or other small talk.

Sometimes I sing when no one is around. I sing Jesus songs that are made up as I'm walking. "*Praise Jesus, Praise Jesus, my savior and my friend, I trust you till the end of time.*" Usually that's as far as I get with the writing of songs, but I sometimes sing it over and over as Elle and I walk.

As I was walking one morning, a car stopped. It was a friend who was looking for her husband who suffered from Alzheimer's. He had wandered off that morning and she couldn't find him. As I continued on my walk the encounter weighed heavy on my mind.

Then as I was walking, a vision came. No, I'm not crazy, but I do have visions, and these visions are always right. In this vision, I could see the lady's husband sitting in a chair chatting with nurses at our nearby hospital. When I got home I quickly contacted the woman and told her what I had seen. Later that day she told me they had found her husband at the hospital. He had told her that he got lost and didn't know where to go, so he walked to the hospital. It was a great relief to know that he had been found safe.

I'm not alone when it comes to having visions. In fact, I believe that most humans have this gift from God. We get so wrapped up in our lives, our world, that we sometimes don't take them seriously. Some people believe that visions come from a spirit guide or angel. I promise you that they only come from God.

Never in my wildest dreams would I imagine that the time I spent walking would result in these amazing stories. The one that I'm about to tell you is my favorite!

I was feeling down and thought a walk would do me good. As I was walking, a lady that I'd seen every now and then approached me. As we started talking she asked if she could pray for me. If you know me, then you know I will never refuse someone praying over me. The fact that another person wants to pray for you is a gift.

This lady began praying and I quickly realized that she was a powerful prayer warrior! Her prayer was one of the most articulate prayers that I'd ever heard.

After the prayer, I commented about it and asked her how she learned to pray like that? She told me simply that she followed Christ and that the Holy Spirit guides her in prayer. *Wow!* All I know is after that prayer I walked away with complete peace. The worries of the day had not disappeared, but I knew that through my faith all would be right.

It also made me think about my prayers and how I pray.

It came to me that prayers need to be specific. Think of it as though you were asking a friend for something. You wouldn't say that you know that thing, that person, I don't know their name, but you know. Your prayers should be surrounded with love for the person that you're praying for, and a prayer needs to be specific, with a name and the reason behind the prayer.

I am a firm believer that God hears each and every prayer that comes from our mouths, but when you're asking God for help in something, even though he's God and knows everything about you, he loves to hear a well thought-out prayer.

Sometimes our prayers don't get answered. I'm not sure why, but I do know without a single doubt that a lot of prayers do get answered and miracles still happen. Don't ever think otherwise.

In the same way, the Spirit helps us in our weakness. We do not know what we ought to pray for, but the Spirit himself intercedes for us through wordless groans.

—ROMANS 8:26

Yearning for God

*T*hroughout my life I've had a yearning for God. It wasn't always recognizable, but I see now that my feeling of missing something was always God.

When I was a young girl I attended Sunday school and sang in the choir, and I remembered loving church. As I got older it didn't seem so important to attend a church or read my Bible, but a tugging on my heart and the feeling of not quite getting my life right was always there. Even though my life was good, I always felt as though something was missing. After dabbling with far-out books, new age beliefs, and countless other mystic ideas, it came to me one day that what I was missing was God.

Once I became a believer and follower of Christ there was no doubt about what had been missing all those years. The truth became crystal clear after I became a born-again follower.

We all tend to reach out and try to find something that

we believe in, something that makes sense, or helps us to understand why we're here and what our purpose is. In fact, you would be hard-pressed to find any human who hasn't had these thoughts at one time or another. Usually a good person feels that they don't need God in their lives. They think, *I'm a good person and treat others with respect and kindness, so why would I need God?* I can answer this, because I was one of those people.

At least I will do my best to answer—it is a challenging thing for me to explain. The best explanation that I have is that once you turn your heart over to God, joy overwhelms your soul, and you feel like a new person. The most exciting moment, the best memory, can't compare to the feelings you have after you ask God to come into your life. This is part of why it's so challenging to explain.

The other reason I believe is because the transformation of becoming a follower of Jesus is filled with supernatural power. If you were to ask yourself what is the perfect life, what would you say that it would take to have it? Achieving a perfect life here on earth and even after this life may not be what you think. You might think that a perfect life is good health and a loving family. This certainly is important in the "perfect life" concept, however I promise you that regardless of your wealth, health, and journey to find the perfect life you will fall short if Christ isn't the top of that list.

When you read God's word you'll start to understand that the words written are not just made-up words. Some would argue that the Bible has been edited and re-worded so many times it just doesn't make common sense in today's world. Others will say that the Bible doesn't apply to today. While some even say that they don't believe in the Bible.

It always makes me sad to hear the latter. Knowing what I know, and how my transformation filled my soul with spiritual perfection it breaks my heart when someone tells me this. Each of us is guided by God, but we don't always know that it's God. Your Father surrounds you with his love, but it's not just any love, it's unconditional love.

There is no fear in love; but perfect love casts out fear because fear has punishment. He who fears is not made perfect in love.

—I JOHN 4:18

Unconditional love doesn't use fear in an attempt to control or coerce. Love protects others and helps calm fears.

Behold, how great a love the Father has bestowed on us, that we should be called children of God! For this cause the world doesn't know us, because it didn't know him.

—I JOHN 3:1 (WEB)

Unconditional love doesn't call names or fixate on flaws. Love sees the potential for the best and hopes for the best in others. Love sees the overlooked, the sad, and the broken and picks them up. It holds them and brings healing and wholeness.

Jesus answered, "I am the way and the truth and the life. No one comes to the Father except through me."

—JOHN 14:6

A Ball of Love

*I*t's hard to imagine ourselves not having a body, but when we die our bodies are no longer needed. Our souls however continue to live. Once our souls descend into heaven, our bodies are no longer needed and the emotions that the soul had on earth change. Think of your soul as a ball of love.

You might think that your soul has pretty much the same feelings when you're dead as it does when you're alive. It does not. In fact, your soul only has the ability to feel one emotion when it no longer resides in your body and that is love. Only love. I'm not sure if a non-believer would have the same experience, but I can safely say through my own experience that if you are a believer of Christ, that the only emotion your soul has is love.

It's hard to imagine this. Loved ones become one, and love rules the next world. In other words, you will know your loved ones in heaven, but you will have the same love for each of them. You won't have more love for one or the other like we sometimes do here on earth.

When you stop to think about it, it's a lot to take in. Really the only thing that is important is that you know God's plan is a perfect one, and there are never any flaws or things that get overlooked. You can trust in him for all things in life as in death.

Bad Christians

*A*lthough a sensitive subject to talk about, it's important that we touch on the thought that not all folks who call themselves *Christians* are living a Christian life or leading by example for true believers.

I look at it like this. I'm not going to allow a fake Christian to spoil my faith. A person who believes in God with all his or her heart has tremendous discernment and the ability to concentrate on the good in most. I for one will never allow anyone to hinder my belief and faith in Christ. My life after this one depends on that. There's always going to be a bad seed, sometimes several, and you might even encounter hundreds during your lifetime. Don't let these types of people determine your future.

When you see them for who they are it will encourage you to stay strong in your faith. However, we shouldn't pass judgment on a fake Christian either. I'm a firm believer that God always has the upper hand, and he will make the final judgment. If we talk about Christians and gossip about others or pass judgment on a so-called Christian who's not living a Christian life, we have just thrown stones at a glass house. This is hard to do, but it's a learning process, and you will find that when you do not judge, you will gain understanding and peace.

We live in a time when the word *Christian* gets a bad rap. You must be the exception to the rule. Don't fall under the evil one's temptations and remain alert to what's really going on. Pray for discernment, and pray for forgiveness if and when you don't turn the other cheek. I think sometimes that when you tell someone you're a Christian they think that you should do no wrong. I'm here to tell you that this is impossible to achieve. However, if you make yourself aware then you will begin to recognize what's really happening.

It is a spiritual battle, and it's happening 24/7. This is why it's important to start every day with the shield of God's armor. There really is such a thing, and I am learning more and more how Satan discourages us and attempts to work in non-Christians to detour us and sway our faith. We must stand firm and tall and not waver. We can do this through God!

You, therefore, have no excuse, you who pass judgment on someone else, for at whatever point you judge another, you are condemning yourself, because you who pass judgment do the same things. Now that we know God's judgment against those who do such things is based on truth. So when you, a mere human being, pass judgment on them and yet do the same things, do you think that you will escape God's judgment? Or do you show contempt for the riches of his kindness, forbearance, and patience, not realizing that God's kindness is intended to lead you to repentance. But because of your stubbornness and your unrepentant heart, you are storing up wrath against yourself for the day of God's wrath, when his righteous judgment will be revealed. God will re-pay each person according to what they have done.

—Romans 2:1-12

We Are All the Same
In the Beginning

*I*f you believe that God is the creator of the universe, then you also believe that he created you. Each of us who are born into this world is created equal in God's eyes. There is not one of us who is better than the other in his eyes.

As we grow and become adults, we sometimes turn away from the teachings of the Bible. Most of us fall over and over only to realize we're repeating the same mistakes. I have been guilty of this time and time again.

Before I became a believer and follower of Christ, it seemed to be easy to repeat bad behavior and habits, but after I became a born-again Christian, it became clear just how bad those decisions and habits were. It became crystal clear that my transformation was not guided by me, but by God. I became a different person! Not only did I become a better human, I also felt the enormous love that God had for me—so much that my heart was filled with his love in a way that I can't put into words.

Becoming a born-again follower of Christ is a miraculous and supernatural event. There is nothing in this world that compares to the experience. The reason is because it comes from God. It's as simple as that!

God watches us mess up over and over as we grow from a child to an adult, but he patiently waits for us to lean on him and call out to him. His everlasting love is unlike any human love that we've ever experienced here on earth.

Your love for Christ is by far the most beautiful love that exists—yesterday, today, and tomorrow. When I became a follower and believer I wanted to shout it from the roof! The transformation of my soul was the most incredible experience that I've ever had! You will discover the same.

How do you ask God to come into your life? Pray this prayer:

Dear Lord Jesus, I know that I am a sinner, and I ask for your forgiveness. I believe you died for my sins and rose from the dead. I turn from my sins and invite you to come into my heart and life. I want to trust and follow you as my Lord and Savior.

When you recite this prayer and it comes sincerely from your heart, God will hear it. I promise. Your life will never be the same. Your thoughts will be centered on

God. Your life will be enriched beyond all of the money in the world. Your friends will notice something different in you. The peace that you now have is beyond anything that you've ever experienced. There will be a skip in your step and a song in your heart.

This is called the Sinner's Prayer. I had never heard it, even though as a child I attended church every Sunday with my family. It all seems so simple, doesn't it? That simple prayer and those powerful words travel from earth to heaven instantly. It puts a whole new meaning into real time!

After you say this prayer and the days to follow come, you will need to refresh your faith by reading the Bible. Even if you read just a few verses, it's important that you stay in God's word. By doing this your faith will remain strong and solid. The world in which we live is going to try and beat you up and spit you out, but you won't be bothered by it. Your faith and trust in the Lord will see you through the worst of times and the best of times.

This is when you really notice the change that has taken place in you. A peace beyond any peace will fill your soul, and fear will no longer be a part of your life. No matter the circumstance or bad experience, your continued faith will protect you and cover you with a perfect blanket of his love. This I know to be true because I have experienced it time and time again.

"Fear not, for I am with you; be not dismayed, for I am your God. I will strengthen you, I will help you, I will uphold you with my righteous right hand."

—ISAIAH 41:10

"...For he has said, 'I will never leave you nor forsake you.' So we can confidently say, 'The Lord is my helper; I will not fear; what can man do to me?'"

—HEBREWS 13:5B-6

For God gave us a spirit not of fear but of power and love and self-control.

—2 TIMOTHY 1:7

Even though I walk through the valley of the shadow of death, I will fear no evil, for you are with me; your rod and your staff, they comfort me.

—PSALM 23:4

"Be strong and courageous. Do not fear or be in dread of them, for it is the LORD your God who goes with you. He will not leave you or forsake you."

—DEUTERONOMY 31:6

"Peace I leave with you; my peace I give to you. Not as the world gives do I give to you. Let not your hearts be troubled, neither let them be afraid."

—JOHN 14:27

The LORD is my light and my salvation; whom shall I fear? The LORD is the stronghold of my life; of whom shall I be afraid?

—PSALM 27:1

God is our refuge and strength, a very present help in trouble. Therefore we will not fear though the earth gives way, though the mountains be moved into the heart of the sea, though its waters roar and foam, though the mountains tremble at its swelling.

—PSALM 46:1-3

Cast your burden upon the LORD and He will sustain you; He will never allow the righteous to be shaken.

—PSALM 55:22

He who dwells in the shelter of the Most High will abide in the shadow of the Almighty. I will say to the LORD, "My refuge and my fortress, my God, in whom I trust."

—PSALM 91:1-2

con·dem·na·tion
\,kän-,dem-'nā-shən-\

The expression of very strong disapproval; censure.
There was strong international condemnation of the attack.

As I read through the Bible I'm reminded that this word was practiced often, but in context, *condemned by God*. Only God can condemn, and it's not our job as Christians to cut someone down for their beliefs or belittle them because they don't believe what we believe.

This is wrong today, and I see it often in churches and areas of ministry. A Christian has a huge responsibility to never condemn. The word itself brings doubt, rejection and confusion. Even when you do not agree with someone, whether it's their lifestyle or method of thinking, the word *condemnation* and *Christian* do not go together. Prayer and reading God's word has the power to stop condemnation in its tracks!

One of the devil's favorite weapons in his bag of dirty tricks is condemnation. This is a hard one to learn, but by being aware of its nature and reading the word of God, you will begin to understand where the source originates. The devil is real, and he's here to rob, steal and destroy your faith in Jesus Christ.

God does not want us to sin, but even if we sin, we will not be condemned because of what Jesus has done for us. The law could not give us eternal life, but God could, and he did it through the death of Christ.

—ROMANS 8:1

The central theme of Romans 8:1-17 is the Spirit. Believers have received the Spirit and, as God's children and joint-heirs with Christ, are to live by the Spirit and not by the corrupted impulses of the flesh.

That sounds easy enough, doesn't it? This is one of the most challenging teachings you will ever learn. The blood of Jesus and his sacrifice on the cross didn't just happen, it was God's perfect plan. The more that you study the Bible the more you'll begin to understand.

I must warn you, however, that when you begin your studies, you will have many light bulb moments! These moments are guided by your understanding of the word and how his perfect love revolves around everything both here on earth and in heaven above. I'm in awe over this! The more I study the Bible the more I become fascinated with it!

To be able to share the message of the cross and how God transformed my life is the most amazing gift. It is designed to be shared with everyone. Not everyone is in agreement with this message. That's okay. It's not our job to convince others if they are in disagreement with our beliefs, however it is our duty to be an example of what a good Christian really is.

It's a lot to take in, but I promise you, your reward will be unimaginable! The reward of trusting and putting your faith in Jesus will exceed anything you've ever experienced. My goal is to share that with as many people as I can.

I want you to have the same peace that I have each and every day. I want you to love life and reap the rewards, as there are many. I want you to live in perfect harmony with God. I want you to share this message too! I want you to turn to God no matter how dire the situation for your answers. I promise you, he will never turn away from you or let you down. He is with you every moment of the day, and as day turns into night, he's right be your side. I imagine God's smile is bigger than any smile I've ever seen!

You Are Beautiful!

You are a creation of the highest God. Don't lose sight of this during difficult or challenging times. Let it be your rock and your foundation to guide you in your decisions and everyday life.

Your faith in God is a gift that will time and time again bring you joy and amazing peace. The gift is not valued by monetary things, but rather this gift holds the highest of value and is priceless and not of this world. As you continue your faith journey, you will discover that you are not the same person that you once were. Until you experience this faith transformation you will have a hard time understanding and possibly even doubt what I've said.

God has given me a gift of a life filled with knowledge and understanding, but this gift is not reserved for me alone. In fact, I believe that God wants *all* of his children to trust and follow him. Do you remember when I said we are all born the same? This gift would have never been recognized had I not known a *before* and an *after.* The *before* has taught me to distinguish the difference between who I once was before becoming a person of faith, and *after*— the transformation is not of this world!

These abilities, often termed "charismatic gifts," are the gifts of knowledge, increased faith, the gift of healing, the gift of miracles, prophecy, the discernment of spirits, diverse kinds of tongues, and interpretation of tongues.

As you walk with God, these abilities will transform your old normal into a tranquil new normal, filled with peace and joy. I can assure you that you've never known this kind of life! You will find that as you practice strengthening your faith it will continue to grow in ways that you never imagine that it would.

Setbacks

It's good to recognize and know where setbacks come from. Our lives are filled with setbacks, illness, death, and the list goes on and on. If you're a born-again Christian, however, these setbacks will not affect you in the way a non-believer experiences them.

You've heard the phrase *bad things happen to good people*. I'm going to tell you without a doubt that bad things, including sickness, despair, and doubt, come from the dark side. Satan's goal is to destroy your faith and cause you to have anxiety and despair. When you become a born-again Christian, you will begin to understand more about how Satan makes every attempt to lead you astray and cause you to doubt your faith in Jesus.

Satan has no power over a born-again Christian and he knows it, however, you must believe that the blood of your Savior, shed when he died at Calvary, released you from the bonds of Satan. Let me say that again. If you're a born-again Christian and you've repented of your sins and asked Jesus into your heart, accepted him as your Lord and Savior, Satan has no power over you. Satan does not have authority over Christ. He never has and he never will. As you read the Bible, you will see how his perfect love and the blood that he shed protects you. How marvelous is that?

There is life in the blood of Jesus; we have no greater protection. There is no greater safety than that of the precious Lamb of Jesus Christ. There is wonder-working power in the blood of the Lamb. You can plead the blood of Jesus over any person or situation. As you and your family are preparing for the day, lay your hands on their heads and say, "In the Name of Jesus, I plead the blood of Jesus over [Jane, Joy, or Jude]."

If you're having trouble on your job or with your co-workers, say, "In the Name of Jesus, I plead the Blood of Jesus over my mind and every individual [call their name if the Spirit leads you] I come into contact with that we walk in divine peace." I like this one as I do it often when I'm in my car: "In the Name of Jesus, I plead the blood of Jesus over this vehicle and all who are going to be with me today. We will go and return in perfect safety."

As you say those words you might feel somewhat unsure. It's important that you believe in Jesus and trust that he is always your protector. If you lose sight or become discouraged, these scriptures are a reminder of his love for you.

But if we walk in the light, as he is in the light, we have fellowship with one another, and the blood of Jesus his Son cleanses us from all sin.

—JOHN 1:7

In him we have redemption through his blood, the forgiveness of our trespasses, according to the riches of his grace.

—EPHESIANS 1:7

Whom God put forward as a propitiation by his blood, to be received by faith. This was to show God's righteousness, because in his divine forbearance he had passed over former sins.

—ROMANS 3:25

He is the propitiation for our sins, and not for ours only but also for the sins of the whole world.

—1 JOHN 2:2

Whoever makes a practice of sinning is of the devil, for the devil has been sinning from the beginning. The reason the Son of God appeared was to destroy the works of the devil.

—1 JOHN 3:8

When Jesus had received the sour wine, he said, "It is finished,"
and he bowed his head and gave up his spirit.

—JOHN 19:30

The Bible is filled with powerful scripture and direction. If we don't read it, we never will understand his perfect plan. As we read the word, we begin to develop this understanding.

My Way

I have come to realize that my way is not usually the best way. The truth is, when I attempt to do things my way, it usually flops, but when I ask God for guidance and pray about my circumstance, no matter how good or bad, I'm filled with a peace and understanding that was previously absent when I did things my way.

What I've learned is that, without God, the outcome is unpredictable. With God, the outcome is predictable. This outcome can be good or bad, but the aftermath of the outcome is perceived differently because of my faith in God. I haven't always thought this way. In fact, for many years I depended on myself for everything. I very seldom asked God to direct me. Occasionally if something really bad happened I'd ask God to help. In fact, when I look back I don't even remember what I asked of God.

Now I talk to him about everything. There isn't a trial or tribulation, a happy moment, a sad moment, that I don't ask God for both direction and guidance. Because I know he's always with me every single second of the day, it's reassuring to know I can ask him for anything.

You might look at my faith as a crutch or a safety net. But I want you to have what I have! I want everyone to have what I have! That is why I've written a book about my faith and how it's changed my life. God wants every single human to have an everlasting life. In truth, we are here on earth for a very short time. No matter what you've done, and no matter how bad it was, you are welcome in the kingdom of God.

Before Lennis passed, I'd thought many times about writing a book. Those thoughts were always on the back burner simmering, but between operating and managing a shop, constant manufacturing and then being a caregiver, time was, well time, and it came and it went. After Lennis passed, it seemed that time slowed down some. Although I was, and am, still busier than ever, God has guided me in a marvelous way to write this book.

I have come to realize that the old saying, *God's time, not my time,* is true, and that his timing is perfect in every way.

It's Not How You Win,
But How You Play
The Game

You've heard this phrase before. When you think of winning a game your mind travels to baseball or possibly that promotion you've always wanted. Winning in life doesn't always live up to those ideas. In fact, it's more about how you play the game.

If you think about it, life is similar to a game. You take chances, you give it your all, and your mind is always centered on winning. Along the way, you get a bonus or a pat on the back. All of these things make you happy, right? Well, they should, but the truth is, they don't always. Why is that? It's easy for me to answer this question because I've lived it.

The truth is happiness comes from gratitude. Gratitude comes from faith, and faith comes from trust. Have you ever met someone who had very little, yet seemed to be the happiest person on earth? My grandmother, Lola, was like this. She lived in a tiny house with very little, yet she always had a smile on her face and kindness in her heart. She was giving and loving, even though she owned few possessions.

She also had a special presence about her. My grandmother had the ability to make a stranger feel at ease and her friends feel loved in this special way. I've come to realize now that my grandmother Lola was one of the wealthiest persons I've ever known. She had what I call the *"God glow."*

Have you ever met someone for the first time and felt that they were special? Maybe it was a twinkle in their eye, or their smile seemed to be contagious. They had a peace about them that stood out. You may not have been able to put your finger on it, but this person made you feel different, and their peace seemed to resonate all around you.

These special souls are rare, and if you're blessed to ever meet one, take your time to talk with them. Do you know what these people have in common? It is God. Their beliefs are centered on God. The decisions that they make are powered by prayer. Their gratitude comes from faith and trust in God. They have the God glow!

I'm not a good person.

You might question that I would even say such a thing, but the truth is I'm not a good person. I strive to be a good person, but there's a battle between good and evil in me each and every day. Who do I blame for this? I blame myself.

Now that I know who's responsible for my bad behavior and thoughts, what do I do to be the person that God wants me to be? I stay in the Word, and the practice of knowing that I can do better, always. Once you begin to train yourself to recognize the evil that lurks within you will begin to have a better understanding of how to become a better person.

You can't do this on your own; you will be required to ask God for guidance and direction as you travel this journey with Christ. There is no psychologist, counselor, or therapist who will be able to make you a better human, only God. You can conquer your doubts, bad thoughts, and bad habits with God.

Rainy Days
& Sunshine

*A*s I walk through my neighborhood on a rainy summer day, I'm reminded of things that probably would not come to mind normally. Elle, my little dog, walks with me, and we often stop for breaks along the way.

This morning as we walked by a home, I noticed there was a for-sale sign in the yard. The only thing that I remember about this house was the old man who lived there once. He always seemed to be alone when we walked by, and often we would see him come out and get his newspaper. He always waved and said hello each and every time that we saw him.

This morning while walking I began to think about the old man who lived in that home. As my mind wandered I realized that the only thing that I remember about him was that he was kind. I knew nothing else about him. These thoughts seemed to build and it led me to understand how not only the old man, but each of us has the ability to either share love or hate. The old man was sharing love, and even though it was a simple wave and hello, he was reaching out to a stranger letting me know that his heart was filled with love.

A simple morning walk in the rain and with it a memory of kindness that at the time had little impact on my day, but on this day the act of kindness has helped me to understand how much we all want to be treated with kindness. We get so wrapped up in our day-to-day living that we sometimes neglect to see the gifts from God that help to make us more like him. This is God's desire, that we become more Christ-like. Forgiving others, treating your neighbor the way you wish to be treated, being kind, not judging. It sounds so easy.

The Transformation

*W*hen you accept Christ's invitation to come into your heart and live in the Spirit you will discover a new you! Suddenly your world will look different and your thoughts will be focused more on God.

In fact, did you know that the invitation to ask God into your life is always sitting on the table of life? From the moment you enter this world until the moments before you depart, the gift of salvation is forever present, but dependant upon your choice and free will.

You might live a lifetime before you accept the invitation. When you decide to accept it, your old life disappears and a bright new one appears. Christ is now living inside you, and you're not the same person you once were.

My life was changed dramatically. Once I became a born-again follower of Christ my worries were few and my heart was light. Oh, I still have life issues just like everyone, but there's now a faith and trust knowing that

God always has my back and he will never abandon me.

There is a catch. God yearns for each of us to study his word on a continuous level. My understanding and experience is that the more I've read the Bible, and made it a priority to practice learning more, the more peace I have. Not just peace, but joy as well.

A non-Christian will always be curious about a Christian. They will notice a difference in you, but are unable to understand what the difference is. You will carry a certain confidence, and when things get tough as they always do, you will start to resonate a sense of peace and understanding like never before.

I'm not going to sugarcoat it and tell you that there will be no struggles and that sadness will disappear. God made each of us human and unfortunately that's part of what we are, but a born-again has an understanding of God's perfect love, and how he wishes to be a part of every decision, and life moment. That includes the good, the bad, and the ugly. I turn to God for each, and have realized and seen that there's no other path I wish to be on. This path is lined with joy, peace, and fulfillment unlike anything that I've ever experienced. I want to share this new understanding of God's love with all. If you're reading this, I want to especially share it with you!

So shall my word be that goeth forth out of my mouth: it shall not return unto me void, but it shall accomplish that which I please, and it shall prosper in the thing whereto I sent it.

—ISAIAH 55-11

The more that I study the Bible and read the word of God, the more understanding I have about the context. Before I was a born-again Christian and when I occasionally read the Bible, it made little sense and seemed complicated and dated. Now when I read the Bible it absorbs deep into my soul.

Always remember, once you become a born-again Christian, you are in this world, but not of it. You now carry Christ in your spirit. He is a part of you now. Your old self is gone and your new self is vibrant and strong. Believe.

When you make this transformation you will notice how the things that were once important to you no longer hold the same value. Maybe you were dependant upon alcohol or drugs, and you needed those things to fulfill your life. Your fulfillment now comes from God, only this fulfillment will far exceed any superficial earthly bandage. You no longer need or want to be patched. You are whole now in mind, body, and spirit in a way that is hard to comprehend because it's not of this world.

Christ is in you and a part of your every moment. Your

choices are now directed by God. He is your teacher and your best friend. Your friends might call you a Holy Roller, and tell you that you're no fun anymore. Remember, you are in this world and not of it. You will begin to discover that nothing compares to this new way of living. Nothing.

Also remember that your friends *will* see a change in you. They won't be able to put their finger on what it is, but they will notice a change. Also remember that your non-believing friends are dependant upon you as an example and you should share God's love for them. *Whew, the pressure is on you!* Just remember it's not your job to change your friends, it's God's, but your born-again newness will compel you to share your faith with your friends. And, I would encourage you to.

Just know that God will always direct you, and offer discernment. Don't put too much pressure on yourself. Just allow God's love to flow through you and the rest will work itself out. Sometimes the outcomes may seem challenging or even wrong, but remember that through prayer, God will never misguide you. You are in good hands when you trust in him.

When you become a born-again follower you're going to get some backlash, and even ridicule from friends and even sometime family. Some of your friends will make attempts to discourage and disappoint you. Stay strong and know that God is by your side.

You may notice that the friends you once had are no longer around. There's a reason for that. Sometimes it will be challenging for non-believers to understand the new you. Although it may seem like they have abandoned you, they have not.

God has a plan for you, and I can promise you it is a better plan then you've ever had for yourself! God will bring new friends into your life, and always remember that your best friend is God. Keep the faith.

A man of many companions may come to ruin, but there is a friend who sticks closer than a brother.

—Proverbs 18:24

If the world hates you, know that it has hated me before it hated you. If you were of the world, the world would love you as its own; but because you are not of the world, but I chose you out of the world, therefore the world hates you. Remember the word that I said to you: 'A servant is not greater than his master.' If they persecuted me, they will also persecute you. If they kept my word, they will also keep yours. But all these things they will do to you on account of my name, because they do not know him who sent me. If I had not come and spoken to them, they would not have been guilty of sin, but now they have no excuse for their sin.

—John 15:18-23

A friend loves at all times, and a brother is born for adversity.
—PROVERBS 17:17

See to it that no one takes you captive by philosophy and empty deceit, according to human tradition, according to the elemental spirits of the world, and not according to Christ.

—COLOSSIANS 2:8

So we do not lose heart. Though our outer self is wasting away, our inner self is being renewed day by day. For this light momentary affliction is preparing for us an eternal weight of glory beyond all comparison, as we look not to the things that are seen but to the things that are unseen. For the things that are seen are transient, but the things that are unseen are eternal.

—2 CORINTHIANS 4:16-18

Fear not, for I am with you; be not dismayed, for I am your God; I will strengthen you, I will help you, I will uphold you with my righteous right hand.

—ISAIAH 41:10

Peace I leave with you; my peace I give to you. Not as the world gives do I give to you. Let not your hearts be troubled, neither let them be afraid.

—JOHN 14:27

In the beginning was the Word, and the Word was with God, and the Word was God.

—John 1:1

For I want you to know how great a struggle I have for you and for those at Laodicea and for all who have not seen me face to face, that their hearts may be encouraged, being knit together in love, to reach all the riches of full assurance of understanding and the knowledge of God's mystery, which is Christ, in whom are hidden all the treasures of wisdom and knowledge. I say this in order that no one may delude you with plausible arguments. For though I am absent in body, yet I am with you in spirit, rejoicing to see your good order and the firmness of your faith in Christ.

—Colossians 2:1-23

"Let not your hearts be troubled. Believe in God; believe also in me. In my Father's house are many rooms. If it were not so, would I have told you that I go to prepare a place for you? And if I go and prepare a place for you, I will come again and will take you to myself, that where I am you may be also. And you know the way to where I am going."

John 14:1-4

Well-Rounded

*H*ave you ever heard the term she or he is *well-rounded*?

The definition of well-rounded is someone who is skilled, capable or knowledgeable in a lot of different things, or something that covers a lot of different areas or subjects. An example of a well-rounded person is someone who is good in school, plays sports and has a good relationship with his family.

They left out the part about how the well-rounded human puts God first. Oh well, we won't hold it against the folks that create the definitions. The reason that I bring this up is simple: I always considered myself to be a "well-rounded" person. That is until I became a believer in Christ. It didn't take very long for me to realize my so-called well-roundedness was lacking, but I could never put my finger on what was missing. I did however know that something was missing.

When I became a born-again follower it became crystal clear that the term has been misunderstood, and that the true meaning should be changed to describe a person who is skilled, capable and knowledgeable in a lot of different things, and carries the love of Christ in their heart. The latter really does make a difference.

In fact, I soon realized after being transformed that my *well-roundedness* was not so well rounded after all until I became a believer and follower. Now my well-roundedness is filled with knowledge and understanding and a sense of knowing. Not an all-knowing, but a knowing that is special and not of this world. A Christ-knowing understanding that my love for Christ is beautiful and filled with perfect love.

Grandma Alexander

I only remember her faintly. My great-grandmother lived on a farm in northern Iowa. I don't remember too much about her, but I do remember that she was a gentle and caring woman. She was soft-spoken and I felt at ease around her from the moment we first met.

I was about six years old when my family visited her Iowa farm. She wore house dresses and black shoes, and her gray hair was always in a bun. Most of the memories that I have are centered on spending time outdoors at her farm. She had pigs, cows, and the coolest river rocks scattered around her property. There was an old red barn right next to a small pig pen. I remember climbing in the fenced pig yard and getting chased by a huge pig!

I don't recall ever being on a farm before, so my experience with farm life was non-existent. Being on that farm was an adventure and I remember feeling like my family was not going to be there long enough for me to explore the way that I wanted to.

To me, Grandma Alexander's farm was something out of a storybook. The land was hilly and filled with river rocks. I remember being fascinated with those rocks even at a young age. One of the treasured rocks sits in my home today! I picked up the large river rock on that day and brought it home. My brother drew a cat on the rock when he was small. It's funny how these memories are strong in my mind and how I've never forgotten them. Of all the memories about my great-grandmother there's one that stands out.

When my grandmother, Christine, was a young girl she lost her baby brother. I don't remember what happened to him but my grandmother was around five or six when he passed. Back then when someone died they would place the body in a casket or on a table in the home and the neighbors and family would pay their respect. My aunt Glenna has shared this story that was passed down by her mother to her, my Grandmother Christine.

This is how the story goes.

It was the middle of August, the hottest month of the year. Little John lay to rest on a large table just off the kitchen. A huge block of ice lay below the table to help preserve his small body while mourners visited him for the last time. My grandmother was bewildered by the adults' behavior, as they would not let her go into the room where her brother's body was being kept. The adults gathered in the kitchen while my great-grandmother Alexander prepared coffee and farm neighbors sat and talked. My grandmother was sitting in the kitchen with the adults and one of the neighbors offered to take her into town to get some candy. The kind man realized that the little girl didn't understand why her brother had died and wanted to take her mind off the tragedy.

When they got home from getting the candy, the adults were still sitting in the kitchen and while they weren't looking she snuck into the room where John's body was laying. She walked up to the table and touched his tiny hand. She told my aunt, her daughter, all those years later how she just wanted to say goodbye to her baby brother. I have tears coming down my cheek as I'm typing this.

The story gets even more soulful.

After little John died my great-grandmother felt lost after losing her precious baby boy. She walked up the hill the day that he passed and sat under an old oak tree. As she was sitting under the tree an angel appeared to her and told her that little John was with God now, and that he was well taken care of. I always thought that this story was fabricated when I was growing up, but I've come to realize that it was not.

It's impossible for any of us to understand the purpose that God has for any death, and even harder to imagine that angels appear, but I now believe that the impossible is the possible. These miraculous things happen all of the time. Not to everyone, but to some.

The story has always touched my heart. As I tell the story it becomes real and is one of my favorite story memories to share. Today, I'm sharing it with you. Little John's body was placed in a white carriage and taken to the country cemetery.

And there were in the same country shepherds abiding in the field, keeping watch over their flock by night. And, lo, the angel of the Lord came upon them, and the glory of the Lord shone round about them: and they were sore afraid. And the angel said unto them, Fear not: for, behold, I bring you good tidings of great joy, which shall be to all people. For unto you is born this day in the city of David a Saviour, which is Christ the Lord. And this shall be a sign unto you; Ye shall find the babe wrapped in swaddling clothes, lying in a manger. And suddenly there was with the angel a multitude of the heavenly host praising God, and saying, "Glory to God in the highest, and on earth peace, good will toward men." And it came to pass, as the angels were gone away…

—LUKE 2:8-15 (KJV)

Be not forgetful to entertain strangers: for thereby some have entertained angels unawares.

—HEBREWS 13:2 (KJV)

The angel of the Lord encampeth round about them that fear him, and delivereth them.

—PSALM 34:7 (KJV)

But ye are come unto mount Sion, and unto the city of the living God, the heavenly Jerusalem, and to an innumerable company of angels,

—HEBREWS 12:22 (KJV)

And there came an angel of the Lord, and sat under an oak which was in Ophrah, that pertained unto Joash the Abiezrite: and his son Gideon threshed wheat by the winepress, to hide it from the Midianites. And the angel of the Lord appeared unto him, and said unto him, "The Lord is with thee, thou mighty man of valour." And Gideon said unto him, "Oh my Lord, if the Lord be with us, why then is all this befallen us? and where be all his miracles which our fathers told us of, saying, 'Did not the Lord bring us up from Egypt?' but now the Lord hath forsaken us, and delivered us into the hands of the Midianites." And the Lord looked upon him, and said, "Go in this thy might, and thou shalt save Israel from the hand of the Midianites: have not I sent thee?" And…

—JUDGES 6:11-24 (KJV)

Angels Among Us

*D*o you believe in angels? I guess it's safe to say that some people do and others don't.

I'm a firm believer that God sends people into our lives and that they are often sent by God as an angel. They may look like us, and be of this world, but these souls are sent from heaven by God for you! You may not always recognize the blessing that these human angels bring until after the encounter, but I can say without any doubt that angels walk among us and bring with them hope, blessings, and most of all love. Sometimes you are given the gift of discernment and are able to recognize that the messenger of the highest God has presented you with an amazing gift.

It was a sunny end of a summer morning and the recent invasion of Covid was wearing me down. I have a lot to say about this illness, but those thoughts will need to be spoken later. For now, let's get back to the story. I awoke starving on that end of summer morning! Even though I was weak, the illness was riding its course and I mustered up enough strength to get in my car and order a very large breakfast. My little dog Elle was with me and we were both sitting in the car waiting for our order when I noticed a homeless lady walking toward my car. I can't explain how, but this lady had *angel* written all over her!

She quickly walked up to my car and began petting Elle. She stood at my car window petting my little dog for at least five minutes. Those moments were filled with supernatural blessings! I told the lady that my dog really liked her, and she smiled the biggest smile. After five minutes of neither of us saying anything, but making eye contact the entire time, I could see the love that this lady carried in her spirit. I almost started crying! That is how moved I was by her encounter.

She told me that she needed to use the restroom and said her goodbyes to my dog. Before she left I said, "God bless you." She looked at me with sincere love and I realized that the emotions that I was feeling were a gift sent to me by a stranger that was down on her luck.

This gift was priceless and helped me to understand the value that every soul has, every person is here on earth for a reason. I'll never forget this encounter, and it encourages me to see that all of us are seeking the same thing: We all want to be loved.

Are not all angels ministering spirits sent to serve those who will inherit salvation?

—HEBREWS 1:14

For he will command his angels concerning you to guard you in all your ways;

—PSALMS 91:11

At the resurrection people will neither marry nor be given in marriage; they will be like the angels in heaven.

—MATTHEW 22:30

Christ Is In You

The moment you become a believer and follower of Christ is the moment that Christ inhabits you. As you follow your faith and study his word you become more Christ-like because he is in you.

When this happens you become more aware of your behavior and will be reminded that Christ does live within you. It's a good thing! It's also a good practice to remind yourself everyday that *Jesus is in you. His Spirit runs through you.* Whenever I'm down or not feeling well I say out loud, *Christ is in me.* Isn't it miraculous to think that God lives in you? My mind is overwhelmed to think about it, but it's true.

Many years of studying the word of God passed before God gave me with this awareness. It was a revelation and life-changing experience when I learned this. Not only will it guide you in making wise decisions in your life, you will have a sense of unearthly peace that cannot be duplicated. You will carry a strong super power and others will recognize that there's something different about you. If they are a follower of Christ they will sometimes recognize this gift, but if they are not they will know that you are different, but not be able to understand it. That's the beauty of being a Christian. Always remember, you are in this world, but not of it. As you grow in your faith, you will begin to have an understanding that you've never had before. Share your new gift with others and tell the world about Jesus. There's not a day that goes by that I don't want to shout to the world the beautiful story of Jesus and his father. A Christian has an obligation to share this knowledge. After all, you want everyone to have what you have, right?

Each of you should use whatever gift you have received to serve others, as faithful stewards of God's grace in its various forms. If anyone speaks, they should do so as one who speaks the very words of God.

—PETER 4:10-11

Go therefore and make disciples of all nations, baptizing them in the name of the Father and of the Son and of the Holy Spirit,

—MATTHEW 28:19

"Judge not, that you be not judged. For with the judgment you pronounce you will be judged, and with the measure you use it will be measured to you. Why do you see the speck that is in your brother's eye, but do not notice the log that is in your own eye? Or how can you say to your brother, 'Let me take the speck out of your eye,' when there is the log in your own eye? You hypocrite, first take the log out of your own eye, and then you will see clearly to take the speck out of your brother's eye...

MATTHEW 7:1-29

As each has received a gift, use it to serve one another, as good stewards of God's varied grace: whoever speaks, as one who speaks oracles of God; whoever serves, as one who serves by the strength that God supplies—in order that in everything God may be glorified through Jesus Christ. To him belong glory and dominion forever and ever. Amen.

—PETER 4:10-11

For I know the plans I have for you, declares the LORD, plans for welfare and not for evil, to give you a future and a hope. Then you will call upon me and come and pray to me, and I will hear you. You will seek me and find me, when you seek me with all your heart.

—JEREMIAH 29:11-13

Reading the Bible

*T*hroughout the Bible there are many verses that stick with me. Some I always turn to in time of need and other times to simply enrich my faith. The scriptures are powerful words for those who believe.

God has given me the wonderful privilege of telling everyone about this plan of his; and he has given me his power and special ability to do his will. Just think! Though I did nothing to deserve it, and though I am the most useless Christian there is, yet I was the one chosen for this special joy of telling the Gentiles the Glad news of the endless treasures available to them in Christ.

May your roots go down deep into the soil of God's marvelous love, and may you be able to feed and understand, as all God's children should, how long, how wide, how deep, and how high his love really is; and to experience this love for yourselves, though it is so great that you will never see the end

143

*of it our fully know or understand it. And so at last you will
be filled up with God himself.*

—EPHESIANS 3:7 & 4:17 (TLB)

Those are powerful words that really make you stop
and think!

As your faith continues to grow through the power
of the Lord, your journey will fill your soul with a peace
that compares to no other. The joy that you carry inside
is from the Holy Spirit, and you will experience the love
that he has for you. His love is above all others, and you
will come to understand this as you dig deeper into the
readings of the Bible.

I've lost track of how many Bibles I have collected over
the years. Each one offers a different take but yet the same
meaning. I often reference a King James Bible, and then
I like to look up the same scripture in both a study Bible
and the Living Bible. All three Bibles allow me to expand
my Bible knowledge.

If you're new to reading the Bible it's probably a good
idea to start with the King James version. You may stumble around some, but you'll find that as you continue to
read you'll begin to understand the words better. The Bible is filled with a variety of men and women who helped
to write it, but the author is God.

Value

*O*ur lives are often filled with sadness and despair. Bad things can happen at the drop of a hat. It has been my experience that no matter what life deals me, I have peace, always. This is the gift that comes from being a faithful believer in Jesus. Death will come to all of us, but knowing that I am going to live forever because of my beliefs puts a completely different perspective on the time that I'm here in this earthly body.

Our future as believers is packed full of supernatural feelings that have no earthly explanation nor should they. When you become a born-again Christian, God's Spirit lives within you. God's plan for you has been in place before you were created. He loves you unconditionally and there is nothing that compares with his love, nothing.

Forgiveness

*O*ne of the most challenging feelings to conquer is forgiveness. We all have experiences where someone has displayed malice or jealousy towards us. This has been a tough one for me to overcome simply because forgiving sometimes feels like giving in.

Before I was a Christ-filled person, it was very difficult for me to forgive. I have realized that I *couldn't* forgive before I became a born-again believer. I have come to understand that forgiving someone who mistreats you is for *you* not for them. Chances are they probably don't even know that they've hurt you. Some people, especially non-believers or people who don't have Christ in their lives, simply don't possess the same amazing peace that you have.

I've experienced jealousy and malice in my own life and have come to learn through the reading of the Bible that it makes no sense to hold onto any feeling that takes away your peace and joy. I also discovered that when you're faced with these types of people on a regular basis it's much harder to forgive them.

It's much easier to forgive when you don't have to be around the people who hurt you. It's much harder when it's a family member or members. Remember, you are a child of the highest God. In his power, you can forgive them. Nevertheless, that doesn't mean that you have to hang out with them. In fact, I've learned that it's best if you don't. When another person is not spirit-filled, they are not going to understand.

There is another answer, too—pray for them. My prayer is always the same: that a person filled with jealousy and malice would ask Jesus into their lives. Once a person becomes a follower of Christ they change in ways that couldn't seem possible. I've also come to realize that when I'm hanging around other believers, I feel more comfortable and safe.

Get rid of all bitterness, rage and anger, brawling and slander, along with every form of malice. Be kind and compassionate to one another, forgiving each other, just as in Christ God forgave you.

—Ephesians 4:31-32

Looking Back

*A*s I look back on my childhood and life I'm constantly reminded of God's protection and amazing grace.

Growing up with a church presence set the tone for my life. I didn't know it at the time, but God did. There was always a feeling that I just wasn't doing enough to fulfill my love for Christ and his teachings.

When a person is searching for a spiritual connection, they sometimes get lost on the wrong track. This was me. I began to dabble in the spirit world before realizing that the spirit world was not what my soul and spirit required to be at peace. Looking back though I realize that I experimented with a number of what I'd call dark forces, because I didn't know the marvelous wonders of my Father and his Son.

In today's society it is acceptable to talk to psychics, dead people and ghosts. Having been one of those people who dabbled in an array of spiritual endeavors, I know first-hand the difference between the Spirit of Christ and the spirit of dark forces. It's hard to distinguish the two when you're wrapped up in anything that is not of God. I'm going to make a lot of psychics angry, but chances are none of them have asked Christ into their lives or they would not be so eager to get involved with these types of dark forces.

One doesn't typically realize or recognize that they're even encountering a dark force unless they are a born-again. I never did. In fact, I always thought that talking to dead people was normal, and that if it could help the living it was a good thing. Boy was I wrong!

As I grew in my faith with Jesus I realized that the things that I once thought were filled with spiritual goodness were the opposite, these things were filled with spiritual darkness. Satan is clever in his ways and is a master deceiver. To some of you this sounds "out there," but to those who are followers of Christ and true believers you know exactly what I'm talking about.

You see, God is a hear-all, see-all God. He knows everything about you. Your thoughts and actions don't go unnoticed and he knows what will happen long before it actually does. God is an all-knowing Father who strengthens us when we call upon him and he comforts us when we need him, regardless of the situation.

A Constant Force

*I*t's been a year since I first started writing this book. Never in my wildest dreams would I have ever imagined the blessing it would be. One of the biggest changes that I see in the span of one year is my faith continues to grow incredibly strong. I've come to realize that without it, my life would not be complete. This will sound strange to a non-believer, but to a believer it will ring true to your heart.

My mind travels to a chapter in the Bible when Peter was asked by Jesus to throw his fishing net one more time.

"Come, follow me," Jesus said, "and I will send you out to fish for people." And he saith unto them, "Follow me, and I will make you fishers of men."

—Matthew 4:19

When I read this scripture I'm reminded of how important it is to teach others about the Bible and how important it is to be a fisher of men and women. The lessons that I've learned in life are valuable, but the lessons that I continue to learn through the Bible are beyond measure of any life lesson.

The son of God is testimony of his love for each of us. His brutal death on the cross was for us then, and thousands of years later, today, and until the end of time. The perfect plan of God has never changed or wavered. It's remained strong and true from the beginning of time.

It's hard to even ponder these thoughts sometimes simply because they are way beyond human comprehension. If we don't understand something we tend to tuck it away and forget it. You will find that once you begin reading the Bible, the words on the page will begin to stand out and make more sense. You will learn how those words feed your soul.

You have the Bible to refresh this new spirit-filled you! Even if you start out reading Psalms a little each day you'll discover that no matter which part of the Bible you decide to read, the impact will be huge. All of this takes place after you ask Christ into your life. The experience will feel overwhelming, but in a way that you've never known. Happiness will follow you and joy will fill your heart.

Trust in Christ

W hen you begin your life as a born-again and place your trust in Christ you will look at distrust and betrayal in a completely different way than you did before you became a follower.

In truth, after you're transformed in Christ there's a good possibility that the friends you once had may not play the same role in your new life. Unless they are believers, you might find it hard to hang out with them. I'm not suggesting that you abandon your old friends and make all new ones, but, and I emphasize the word *but*, you are going to find that your thoughts and feelings about things have changed. Not in a bad way, but in a supernaturally good way! Your non-Christian friends might see it differently. They sometimes will believe that you have snubbed them. This is a common occurrence with a born-again person.

I'll share a personal story about this.

Before I became a believer, my lifestyle centered on having a good time, which included weekends having a few cocktails and indulging in alcohol. I was not a heavy drinker. In fact, I would consider myself to be a moderate drinker, if that.

When I became a born-again Christian, my lifestyle changed. It wasn't as though I had a problem with alcohol and needed to stop drinking, but rather drinking just didn't feel like something that I wanted to do. After I stopped hanging out with friends who drank, I realized that I was content and happier not drinking.

After this change in my life I noticed something. My friends who drank didn't want to hang out with me. I guess they considered me to be a stick in the mud. A few months into my new way of life I had a good friend tell me that I wasn't fun anymore. I realized that her idea of fun was centered on drinking, and I no longer felt that I needed to drink to have fun.

I didn't experience peer pressure or feelings of guilt after my friend said that, but a complete sense of peace and happiness. This was not because of my own thoughts, but the Spirit of Christ, who now lived inside me.

How marvelous this place will be! However, only those whose names are written in the Book of Life can enter and stay in this wonderful place.

REVELATION 21:27

It's hard to imagine having another life beyond the one that I have, but when you turn your heart over to Jesus and trust in him for all things you also receive another amazing gift, and that gift is everlasting life. It's hard to imagine living forever; at least my mind can't grasp those thoughts. Forever is wrapped up with love and learning and sharing, and I would imagine other supernatural things that my mind can't imagine. It is beyond anything I can imagine.

The Journey

*T*hroughout our lives, each of us experience happy moments as well as sad and challenging times. In fact, it's safe to say that each day presents trials and unpredictable moments, and we never know what can happen next.

When you're a follower or believer, your thoughts are centered on God. Each of us travels a different life journey, but when you're front and center with God, and trust in him with all of your heart, your journey is the same as every fellow follower. Followers of Christ are on the same journey. They yearn to learn more about Jesus, and they are eager to read the Bible and expand their faith though the word of God.

It's interesting how a year ago when I first started writing this book, these beliefs guided and instructed me in ways that I just didn't understand then. But now, a year later, my faith has grown and is much stronger than it was when I first started this book. It's hard for me to imagine that my faith would become stronger, because I felt like it was solid and unwavering. Through daily prayer and the thirst to learn more, I have realized that, even though my faith was strong a year ago, it continues to grow as I gain new knowledge from reading the Bible.

It's wonderful to know that this book that has been around for thousands of years is filled with vast knowledge and understanding of the world.

Keep on loving each other as brothers and sisters. Don't forget to show hospitality to strangers, for some who have done this have entertained angels without realizing it! Remember those in prison, as if you were there yourself. Remember also those being mistreated, as if you felt their pain in your own bodies.

Give honor to marriage, and remain faithful to one another in marriage. God will surely judge people who are immoral and those who commit adultery.

Don't love money; be satisfied with what you have. For God has said, "I will never fail you. I will never abandon you."

So we can say with confidence, "The LORD is my helper, So I will have no fear. What can mere people do to me?"

Remember your leaders who taught you the word of God. Think of all the good that has come from their lives, and follow the example of their faith.

Jesus Christ is the same yesterday, today, and forever. So do not be attracted by strange, new ideas. Your strength comes from God's grace, not from rules about food, which don't help those who follow them.

—HEBREWS 13

That is worthy of repeating: *Jesus Christ is the same yesterday, today, and forever.*

Your journey though Christ is not so different than mine. We are guided by God with an understanding of this as we read scripture. That blows me away! We have been given an amazing gift, the Bible!

Word of Mouth

*H*aving been a business owner for over twenty-five years, I have grown to understand the value of word-of-mouth and consider it a valuable marketing tool. It's even more effective than social media marketing, television or radio.

Since I've done all of those things, it's fair for me to tell you this. The same goes for spreading the word about Jesus. I've come to realize that the most important thing that I will ever do is to tell others about the wonderful world of Christ. Not only does it fulfill me in ways that can't be put into words, it also is my duty.

Once a person becomes a born-again it's important to tell others about your amazing transformation and how they too can experience the spiritual peace of knowing God and having a personal relationship with him. Not all will accept this new knowledge, but some will. This is why it's important to share your faith with others and your knowledge of Christ. When you do, you'll notice an overwhelming feeling of joy like you've never felt before.

As a believer and follower of Christ, I want everyone to have everlasting life. I yearn for all to be included in the Book of Life. Before you walk out on the street and begin spreading the good word, it's wise to pray for discernment. One thing I've learned about God and his faithful guidance is that when we pray for discernment, he responds with direction and answers, always.

For the wages of sin is death, but the free gift of God is eternal life in Christ Jesus our Lord.

—Romans 6:23

For by grace you have been saved through faith. And this is not your own doing; it is the gift of God, not a result of works, so that no one may boast.

Ephesians 2:8-9

Jesus said to him, "I am the way, and the truth, and the life. No one comes to the Father except through me."

—John 14:6

No one who abides in him keeps on sinning; no one who keeps on sinning has either seen him or known him. Little children, let no one deceive you. Whoever practices righteousness is righteous, as he is righteous. Whoever makes a practice of sinning is of the devil, for the devil has been sinning from the beginning. The reason the Son of God appeared was to destroy the works of the devil. No one born of God makes a practice of sinning, for God's seed abides in him, and he cannot keep on sinning because he has been born of God. By this it is evident who are the children of God, and who are the children of the devil: whoever does not practice righteousness is not of God, nor is the one who does not love his brother...

—1 JOHN 3:6-11

And Peter said to them, "Repent and be baptized every one of you in the name of Jesus Christ for the forgiveness of your sins, and you will receive the gift of the Holy Spirit."

—ACTS 2:38

But nothing unclean will ever enter it, nor anyone who does what is detestable or false, but only those who are written in the Lamb's book of life.

—REVELATION 21:27

Jesus answered him, "Truly, truly, I say to you, unless one is born again he cannot see the kingdom of God."

—JOHN 3:3

Practice What You Preach

*A*lmost everyone has heard the phrase: *Practice what you preach.* I've often wondered where that popular phrase originated.

So practice and observe whatever they tell you—but not what they do. For they preach, but do not practice.

—MATTHEW 23:3

After you accept Jesus, God will guide you, but you'll need to stay in the word and practice what you preach. It will not be easy at times, but it will fulfill your soul and complete your spirit. You might feel as though you've discovered a worldly secret. You have! Just as a person studies for a test or speech, studying the truths of the Bible will expand your understanding and impacts this life as well as the next one.

What causes quarrels and what causes fights among you? Is it not this, that your passions are at war within you? You desire and do not have, so you murder. You covet and cannot obtain, so you fight and quarrel. You do not have, because you do not ask. You ask and do not receive, because you ask wrongly, to spend it on your passions. You adulterous people! Do you not know that friendship with the world is enmity with God? Therefore whoever wishes to be a friend of the world makes himself an enemy of God. Or do you suppose it is to no purpose that the Scripture says, "He yearns jealously over the spirit that he has made to dwell in us"? ...

—JAMES 4:1-17

You are now in this world, but not of it. The world we live in is temporary, but if you are a believer and follower, your life after this one is eternal. You will find it difficult to evaluate and understand just exactly how long forever is. The mere thought of forever boggles my mind, and frankly I don't spend a lot of time thinking about it. I do however yearn to spend time expanding my knowledge and understanding of the Bible and its amazing gift of words.

The world it is a changing.

It doesn't take me very long to realize how much our world and the ways of the world have changed just in my lifetime. The good old days of hiking alone in the woods or spending summer days riding bikes in the small town that I grew up in are gone. This makes me extremely sad. The era in which I grew up will probably never come back. But I also know that this time we live in is an opportunity to refine our knowledge of God.

Now more than ever, we need God in our lives. Not just here and there, but every second, every minute of the day. When everything seems to toss and turn and head upside down like it often does nowadays, devotion to God is gift and a blessing. It not only helps us to stay grounded but it also offers peace. Your world can change at the drop of a hat, but your consistent faith and trust in Jesus should never change.

You will find that the more you study and read the Bible the more your faith will continue to grow in unimaginable ways that far exceed anything you ever imagined. That is the supernatural Spirit of God working in you. Not only will he help you in overcoming fear and anxiety, he will also comfort you in times of despair. No human being can comfort you the way that God can. When you call upon the Lord, he is there, always. This I promise.

You may be eager to see something change quickly or turn around, but sometimes it doesn't. You may wonder why God hasn't intervened and turned a situation into something that pleases you. I've come to realize that God does not work like this. Since he's an all-knowing God he has the gift of seeing things play out long before they happen.

I can promise you this—God will never let you down. If you believe in him and trust in him, he will always, without fail, have your back. Don't allow Satan to convince you otherwise. He will do his best to discourage you and convince you that God is not important.

Plant healthy seeds of faith and spread them—so that faith is cultivated and nourished.

As for me, I shall call upon God, And the LORD will save me. Evening and morning and at noon, I will complain and murmur, And He will hear my voice. He will redeem my soul in peace from the battle which is against me, for they are many who strive with me. God will hear and answer them— even the one who sits enthroned from of old. With whom there is no change, and who do not fear God.

PSALMS 55:16-19

Loving God

*A*s I look back on my childhood I realize that I've always loved God. I have fond memories of my mom and dad sitting with me in church, and going to Sunday school class before church started. Even as a little girl I recall sitting on the church pew staring at the wondrous stain glass windows. I sang in the choir and loved it!

As I got older and became an adult I realized that my love for God was not an accident. If you believe that God knows all, then you must also believe that he knows your future. There has always been a yearning in me to know more about God and understand the Bible.

When I became a born-again by asking Jesus to come into my heart and forgive me of my sins, my life became new. Hence the phrase, born again.

Asking God to come into your heart is one of the easiest things you'll ever do, but the results that your spirit obtains through your salvation far exceed anything you'll ever encounter in your lifetime. I can honestly tell you this, because I'm living proof.

God will guide you in all that you do. You trust God to help you make decisions. You pray about difficult times and you are comforted by his continual love and faithful support in all that you do here on earth.

It's interesting how before I became a faithful servant I only prayed to God when things weren't going my way. Nowadays, I pray each day regardless of my situation. If things are good, I pray, and if things are bad, I pray. I tell God that I love him, and I thank him for every day. Those thoughts come from the deepest of my heart.

That's one thing you'll notice when you turn your heart over to God, you will discover that your prayers and thoughts feel rooted in his love and truth. Those healthy god-fearing roots bring joy to God's heart not only through you prayers but through your actions.

One of the hardest things you'll ever do is be a true Christian. Today's world is filled with evil in every shape, form, and corner. We need God more than ever in our world to combat the constant evil that surrounds us. No matter the situation, you no longer depend on your own answers, you depend only on God's. Believe me when I tell you that he's got your back, always.

Angels

*I*f you read the Bible and have read scripture regarding angels then you know that angels are angels and humans are humans. I'm afraid that I'm going to lose some of you with this one, but I speak the truth of the Bible in regards to angels. According to the Bible, we do however each have a guardian angel, but when a loved one passes, they do not turn into an angel. God created angels and he created humans. He chose you to be a human.

...but the angel of the LORD called to him from heaven and said, "Abraham, Abraham!" And he said, "Here I am."

—Genesis 22:11

For the Son of man shall come in the glory of his Father with his angels; and then he shall reward every man according to his works.

—Matthew 16:27

Not all angels are faithful servants of God. Fallen angels, also known as demons, were angels who rebelled against God, and were cast out of heaven for their disobedience. Revelation 12:7-9 says that a third of the angels fell from heaven when they followed Satan.

Behold, I send an angel before you to guard you on the way and to bring you to the place that I have prepared.

—EXODUS 23:20

For he shall give his angels charge over thee, to keep thee in all thy ways.

—PSALM 91:11

For he will command his angels concerning you to guard you in all your ways. On their hands they will bear you up, lest you strike your foot against a stone.

—PSALM 91:11-12

Do not neglect to show hospitality to strangers, for thereby some have entertained angels unawares.

HEBREWS 13:2

Just so, I tell you, there is joy before the angels of God over one sinner who repents.

—LUKE 15:10

So it will be at the close of the age. The angels will come out and separate the evil from the righteous.

—MATTHEW 13:49

And no wonder, for even Satan disguises himself as an angel of light.

—2 CORINTHIANS 11:14

Are not all angels ministering spirits sent to serve those who will inherit salvation?

—HEBREWS 1:14

Dear friends, do not believe every spirit, but test the spirits to see whether they are from God, because many false prophets have gone out into the world.

—1 JOHN 4:1

Thou believest that there is one God; thou doest well: the devils also believe, and tremble.

—JAMES 2:19 KJV

BIBLES, BIBLES

*A*while back you might recall my miraculous story
about how I had a vision about the lost Bible of
my childhood. It was my first Bible! The vision was clear
and precise and left me without any doubt as to where
that dedicated Bible was some fifty years later.

In the vision, I saw my childhood Bible sitting on a
shelf amongst other Bibles in the basement of the church
that I attended as a young girl. I knew without a shadow
of any doubt this vision was real. As I'm typing, it sits in
my office drawer. It's tattered and torn but has my name
engraved on the cover.

My point of this story is, first of all, always trust your
instincts and listen to the voices in your head. Well sometimes! All joking aside, I believe that God speaks to you
often. If you're a born-again you'll know exactly what I'm
referring to.

While I'm on the subject of Bibles, I'd like to touch on

the importance of having in your possession different versions of Bibles. For example, I read from King James, The Living Bible, and even a children's Bible. I love to have a better understanding of the scripture. Reading a number of different Bible translations can sometimes aid in your understanding.

The translations are similar, but sometimes The Living Bible is easier to read and understand. If you're like me and interested in learning more from God's word, I encourage you to expand your Bible knowledge by reading different translations.

Some time ago, I read Hebrews 10-13 and was blown away by the words:

The old system of Jewish laws gave only a dim foretaste of the good things Christ would do for us. The sacrifices under the old system were repeated again and again, year after year, but even so they could never save those who lived under their rules. If they could have, one offering would have been enough; the worshipers would have been cleansed once for all and their feeling of guilt would be gone. But just the opposite happened: those yearly sacrifices reminded them of their disobedience and guilt instead of relieving their minds. For it is not possible for the blood of bulls and goats really to take away sins.

That is why Christ said as he came into the world, "O God, the blood of bulls and goats cannot satisfy you, so you have made ready this body of mine for me to lay as a sacrifice upon your altar. You were not satisfied with the animal sacrifices, slain and burnt before you as offerings for sin. Then I said, 'See, I have come to do your will, to lay down my life, just as the Scriptures said that I would.'"

After Christ said this about not being satisfied with the various sacrifices and offerings required under the old system, he then added, "Here I am. I have come to give my life."

He cancels the first system in favor of a far better one. Under this new plan we have been forgiven and made clean by Christ's dying for us once and for all.

—HEBREWS 10 (TLB)

Please continue to read, it will draw light on what God did for each of us. You will come away with a grateful heart.

Our People

*T*here are times when I stop and think about the couple that raised me, my amazing parents, and my mind is boggled with thankfulness to God. My mom has been gone for awhile, but my dad is still around and I'm forever grateful that he is. My life would never be what it is today without the love and compassion of my dad.

I've always believed that God chooses our parents. The parents that you have are not random, they're chosen. They are your people! Sometimes they might differ in beliefs, while other times you may have gotten a bad hand and have parents that are selfish and unbelievers. There's a reason they're your parents, regardless of the situation or their personality.

I've witnessed this first hand and always compared other's parents with my own only to realize just how blessed I have been in life. It's hard for me to imagine not having a loving and caring parent because I've never experienced it, but I know that it happens. Let me first say, your parents do not determine how you're going to live your life. That is entirely up to you and, of course, God.

It's hard to believe that dire and extreme situations happen for a reason. If you are a believer of Christ then you must remember this and hold fast to that thought. When life is at its bleakest, God will shine his light the brightest. I promise you.

You've heard that old saying—*no one comes into your life by accident.* I have learned that this is not only true, but the hard lessons that I've learned have molded me and shaped my faith to be stronger. Sometimes people come into your life to help teach you a lesson, while other times, their presence might be short and sweet. When I stop and think about this the more I've come to realize that it's not only true, but a gift. These encounters are an amazing gift from God.

Whether they be sad lessons, or challenging ones they are lessons, and unless you live on a remote island, you are going to encounter both friend and foe during the course of your life here on earth. If you stop to think, you'll tend to look at mishaps and unusual encounters for what they are, and you'll understand that God has sent this person into your life for a reason.

I've had some interesting encounters at my shop. The

stories of meeting strangers when you least expect it is an interesting story. Here's one that stands out:

A few years ago while I was working at my shop, a couple came in. They were Japanese. I asked them how they happened upon my shop. They replied that they weren't sure. They took the exit not planning to, they said, and then parked downtown, and came directly to my shop. As we began talking, I began to casually bring up that I was a Christian. They in turn told me that they were Christians, too.

If you know anything about Japan, then you know that approximately one percent of Japan's population is Christian. What are the odds of strangers who reside in Japan happening into my shop? I would say the odds are against both of us. However, there are no such things as coincidences with God, the odds are always in his favor.

I began chatting with the couple about God, and before I knew it, we were having a revival in my shop. All three of us were sharing our testimonies and how God had come into our lives. The couple explained how their parents were Christians, and shared their love for Christ throughout their childhood.

One of my favorite things to ask other Christians is, *what has Jesus done for you?*

My stories and the testimonies of others are supposed to be shared. Before being a born-again, my life was void in many ways. Even though I had a great life, it felt as though something was missing. Until I became a born-again, I couldn't grasp the changes that have taken place. Each change gradually fills my spirit with happiness unlike any happiness I've ever encountered. I want to share this with everyone so that you can experience it too. I actually want to shout it through the roof, but I know that's not a realistic thought. I would like to say that when you turn your heart over to God, both you and your life will take a golden turn.

Dear brothers, is your life full of difficulties and temptations? Then be happy, for when the way is rough, your patience has a chance to grow. So let it grow, and don't try to squirm out of your problems. For when your patience is finally in full bloom, then you will be ready for anything, strong in character, full and complete. If you want to know what God wants you to do, ask him, and he will gladly tell you, for he is always ready to give a bountiful supply of wisdom to all who ask him; be sure that you really expect him to tell you, for a doubtful mind will be as unsettled as a wave of the sea that is driven and tossed by the winds, and every decision you then make will be uncertain, as you turn first this way and that. If you don't ask with faith, don't expect the Lord to give you any solid answer.

—JAMES 1:2-6

Strength in Faith

I've been thinking about where my strength comes from. We all need strength in our lives, and sometimes it's hard to gather it when we're faced with difficult situations or challenges. Before I was a born-again Christian, I depended solely upon my own strength to carry me through everything, but when I was born again, I realized that my strength comes from God.

He always, without fail, is present and even knows what's going to happen before it even happens. So whatever comes your way, be it good or bad, he's in control. It's hard for some to comprehend that because it's supernatural, but it's true! Well of course it is, it comes from God!

When we turn our trust over to him completely, without any doubt, and joyfully trust in him, he takes the reigns and builds our strength to a degree that is supernatural. It's one of the most beautiful things that I've ever experienced. You've heard the phrase "there is strength in numbers." Ditch that, and replace it with *there is strength in God!*

We live in the shadow of the Almighty, sheltered by the God who is above all gods.

This I declare, that he alone is my refuge, my place of safety; he is my God, and I am trusting him. For he rescues you from every trap and protects you from the fatal plague. He will shield you with his wings! They will shelter you. His faithful promises are your armor. Now you don't need to be afraid of the dark anymore, nor fear the dangers of the day; nor dread the plagues of darkness, nor disasters in the morning.

Though a thousand fall at my side, though ten thousand are dying around me, the evil will not touch me. I will see how the wicked are punished, but I will not share it. For Jehovah is my refuge! I choose the God above all gods to shelter me. How then can evil overtake me or any plague come near? For he orders his angels to protect you wherever you go. They will steady you with their hands to keep you from stumbling against the rocks on the trail. You can safely meet a lion or step on poisonous snakes, yes, even trample them beneath your feet!

For the Lord says, "Because he loves me, I will rescue him; I will make him great because he trusts in my name. When he calls on me, I will answer; I will be with him in trouble and rescue him and honor him. I will satisfy him with a full life and give him my salvation."

—Psalm 91

But he said to me, "My grace is sufficient for you, for my power is made perfect in weakness." Therefore I will boast all the more gladly about my weaknesses, so that Christ's power may rest on me. That is why, for Christ's sake, I delight in weaknesses, in insults, in hardships, in persecutions, in difficulties. For when I am weak, then I am strong.

—2 Corinthians 12:9-10

Whoever dwells in the shelter of the Most High will rest in the shadow of the Almighty. I will say of the Lord, "He is my refuge and my fortress, my God, in whom I trust."

—Psalm 91:1-2

The Importance of Powerful Prayer

Whether you're a believer or a non-believer, you have encountered challenging times. Often in these times believers tell you that they will pray for you. The truth is, and I'm speaking personally, those words sometimes feel empty. I'm not telling you this to discourage you, but I'm just being honest. I just don't feel it sometimes.

I also hear people request prayer, but not specifically list a name or a reason for the prayer. What I've learned is that prayer is a powerful weapon against the enemy. I also believe that prayer is not just saying a few words and expecting God to answer. Of course, we would like to think that all of our prayers will be answered by God, and they are, but it's always God's timing, and sometimes he calls people home. I don't claim to have all of the answers, but I do believe that God has shown me how significant prayer is and that there is a proper way of doing it.

I know what you're thinking. Prayer is prayer. If you pray for someone, no matter the style or matter in which you pray is irrelevant to God. He is going to hear your prayer. I'm afraid that I disagree with this. When you pray for someone, you need the facts of their ailment or worldly challenge so that your prayer is strong and powerful.

I compare it to talking on the phone and explaining to a friend exactly and precisely what took place to describe an incident. You wouldn't leave out significant points as you explain the situation. If so, your story might not be heard correctly. It's easy to believe that an all-knowing God doesn't need to know the specifics when we pray. After all, if you read a few chapters back you know that God is an all-knowing God. He knows everything including the good, the bad, the ugly, the unexpected, the past, and the future. I absolutely believe this, but when it comes to calling on God in prayer, he wants us to pray with intention and specifics.

One of the hardest things I've ever done is to pray for someone who has mistreated me or showed malice. It's not something that comes easy to anyone, regardless of whether you believe in God or not. The truth is that by faith, he will shine down on you and help you to understand and have empathy for the people that have done you wrong. Not only does it free you, but it also fills your spirit with true forgiveness. By the way, I've never been able to perform this miraculous process without God's help.

Before bed and when I say my prayers, they are always specific. I don't just pray for my family and friends, I pray for good health, but those health prayers are specific. I pray that my brother's mind is strong and that his organs, heart, lungs, kidneys, etc. are strong and healthy. I even pray for my mom and my grandmother. Both are gone, but I pray that they are happy in heaven. Every night I say these powerful prayers.

If a friend has overcome cancer, I pray that cancer will never come back and that their organs are strong and healthy. That an old person has the mind of a twenty-year-old. Do you see the difference in prayer? In other words, I try to completely cover the bases when I pray.

Sometimes our prayers don't get answered and that's a tough pill to swallow. The enemy would love for you to stop believing in God because your prayers weren't answered. God wants you to remain strong in faith and trust him. He will reward you for your steady unwavering faith. Let me say that one more time. I promise that God will reward you when you remain strong in faith.

So the next time you pray for someone, practice authority over your prayer. Be specific in your requests to God. He already knows the outcome, but never forget that he's a loving God and does not have the ability to hurt you, but rather his pure love is unearthly and supernatural.

Dreams

And the dream was repeated to Pharaoh twice because the thing is established by God, and God will shortly bring it to pass.

—GENESIS 41:32 (NKJV)

And for that the dream was doubled unto Pharaoh twice; it is because the thing is established by God, and God will shortly bring it to pass.

—GENESIS 41:32 (KJV)

I believe that God speaks to us in our dreams. Many years ago before re-opening my shop I felt that my future was uncertain. It's really the only time in my life that I've felt this.

My mom had passed a few years before, and I had been a caregiver for several years. I really just didn't know what I should be doing in life. I'd taken some time off and only had my shop open in my home on Saturdays. The notion of opening my shop again downtown had entered my mind only to be quickly dissolved with logic. I might add my own logic. I felt strongly about not wanting to open a shop again. All of the work involved and the time spent sitting at a shop just didn't appeal to me.

We all encounter feelings of uncertainty at some point in our lives. That night I prayed and asked God to tell me what I should be doing, and I had the wildest dream. First of all, it was what is referred to as a lucid dream. When you have a lucid dream you are aware that you are dreaming. I'd never experienced a lucid dream before, and it felt unique and special since I'd not even tried to have one. In a lucid dream, you're in control of your dream. You can navigate the dream in the direction that you want it to go.

In my dream, I dreamt that I was once again a shop owner. I was happy-go-lucky in this dream. I was in my shop arranging flowers. I remember that I was able to change the color of the flowers in my dream. It was as simple as saying red flowers turn blue, and presto they were blue! Since I was aware that I was dreaming, it was the most fascinating dream that I've ever encountered. I woke the next morning with excitement and eagerness to be a shop owner once again. I was determined to find a spot for my shop that next day. I drove downtown and circled around the square only to be disappointed. There were no open spaces available. I came home discouraged and deflated, but that dream was hanging on to every other thought.

That night I had the same dream continued! It was another lucid dream. What are the odds? I was even dancing and singing as I walked across my shop floor. The next morning when I woke I said out loud, *I get it, God.* The overwhelming feeling to open a shop was tugging at me in every way that it could. I once again drove downtown to search for a good spot to open a shop. There was nothing to be had! Once again discouragement and dismay filled my heart.

A month or so later I was meeting with a friend for lunch. We spent hours catching up. My friend owned a shop downtown in an old house. As we were getting ready to leave, I mentioned my dream to her. She said it's funny that you tell me about this dream because I've been thinking of asking you if you'd be interested in having a small space in my shop.

What! What! I even said out loud, "What!" We started chatting a bit more, and within a few months, I found myself walking across my new shop floor, dancing and singing while placing blue flowers in a vase. Later, after I studied scripture, I realized the significance of the dream being repeated. The Bible talks about it. To make the story even more interesting, the location where my friend had her shop was my old location. I was returning to my original shop location.

As for having two similar dreams, it means that these events have been decreed by God, and he will soon make them happen. In Genesis 41, you'll read how Pharaoh had two similar dreams. The Bible is filled with stories about dreams. Sometimes dreams are delivered by God when you don't ask.

Recently I had a dream that was centered on forgiveness. It was an ordinary night. I watched a movie and said my prayers, but some time in the middle of the night, I had a supernatural experience that was centered on forgiveness. I woke up the next morning as a different person! I no longer hung onto the challenge of forgiving the ones who had hurt me. I believe that God gave me the spirit of forgiveness.

In my dream, I accepted the amazing gift of forgiveness from God and now carry the spirit of forgiveness. Since we are human, we are not equipped to easily forgive. I'm guilty of it, and so are you. It's part of being a human being, but it doesn't have to be. What would you say if I told you that you can rid yourself of not being able to forgive those who have done you wrong? You can overcome and experience forgiveness with the power of God. I know because I've experienced it! Like many gifts from God, its supernatural in nature and one would be hard-pressed to explain.

It makes sense to me that we are filled with a variety of spirits. Not the kind you're probably thinking though. These spirits are in all of us. There's the spirit of fear, and doubt, and one of the biggest ones is not being able to fully forgive. They're all hard to take on yourself, but through the power of the Almighty, you can overcome any negative spirits who try to take up residence in you. The amazing part is all that is required is that you ask God. Do you remember when I spoke about specific prayer? It's very similar to gaining the spirit of forgiveness.

Let's get back to my dream. Remember, if a dream is continued, it is often from God, and he's working in you and with you in your dreams.

I actually had two dreams. The first was a dream, but it wasn't. I know I'm going to really need to explain that! In my dream, or slumber state let's call it, God filled me with the spirit of forgiveness. I woke up and was in awe over how I felt. Not being able to explain what had happened, but knowing that I felt different, I went back to sleep and the same feelings that were associated with the slumber turned into a dream.

In the dream, I was making bonbons. I know right? As I got ready to complete the final touches on the bonbons by rolling them in powdered sugar, God intervened and told me not to roll them in the sugar. He told me that the bonbons were not finished, and that was a metaphor for how I had been handling forgiveness. No matter how hard I tried to forgive, sometimes it just wasn't enough. In my heart I always forgave, but the spirit of unforgiveness was alive and living within me.

Now I realize that not everyone experiences something like what I experienced, but I do believe without a shadow of any doubt that our Father God is the only one who has the ability to help us overcome and conquer the ability to completely forgive. Once you have one of these supernatural experiences you will never think the same way. Your heart will be light and your spirit will be filled with an all-understanding of God's love and how important it is to him that we forgive. It's a spectacular feeling to be able to willingly forgive.

Then Peter came up and said to him, "Lord, how often will my brother sin against me, and I forgive him? As many as seven times?" Jesus said to him, "I do not say to you seven times, but seventy-seven times." Therefore the kingdom of heaven may be compared to a king who wished to settle accounts with his servants. When he began to settle, one was brought to him who owed him ten thousand talents. And since he could not pay, his master ordered him to be sold, with his wife and children and all that he had, and payment to be made...

—MATTHEW 18:21-35 (ESV)

And whenever you stand praying, forgive, if you have any-thing against anyone, so that your Father also who is in heaven may forgive you your trespasses."

—Mark 11:25 (ESV)

Bearing with one another and, if one has a complaint against another, forgiving each other; as the Lord has forgiven you, so you also must forgive.

—Romans 12:19 (ESV)

Beloved, never avenge yourselves, but leave it to the wrath of God, for it is written, "Vengeance is mine, I will repay, says the Lord."

—Mark 11:25 (ESV)

For if you forgive others their trespasses, your heavenly Father will also forgive you.

—Matthew 6:14 (ESV)

The Bible is filled with forgiveness scripture. Its words are powerful and true.

Don't Place God in a Box

Sometimes we try to put God in a box. You have to remember God is the creator of all things, everything. That blows me away! Putting restrictions on him and doubting his word is like saying that you don't believe.

Often we are filled with doubt that God can't handle a dire situation. You've heard me say before how the enemy is always around to kill, steal, and destroy, but that doesn't mean you need to worry. In fact, once you become a born-again you're going to find that Satan tries to wiggle his evil worm into your life every chance he gets.

Now that I'm a born-again I'm able to recognize his disguises most of the time. But keep in mind, he's tricky. The good news is that God has him by the leash and is in control of all situations. It's important to remember this, especially when hard times come.

We sometimes consider God a supernatural being who

is untouchable. In fact, nothing could be farther from the truth. God has one goal for you and one goal only: That you believe in him with all of your heart, and that you share his word with everyone. I know what you're thinking. Some people will turn away and think that you've lost it. Think about that for a moment. Satan's greatest fear is that your faith remains strong and you share it with others. I believe that is the sole purpose of why we're here.

When I stop and think about how short my life is here on earth, I can't help but also ponder what my purpose is. I know you've thought about that. I believe it's safe to say that we all have. For me, even though I practiced good works and believed in God, I rarely shared my beliefs with others. Well I take that back. I openly shared my beliefs with others in a casual sense.

Remind yourself that God can't be put into a box. He's an all-knowing and loving Father that always has your best interests at heart. We may be able to put humans in a box and limit their abilities, but there is no way we will ever be able to put God in a box.

So then faith comes by hearing, and hearing by the word of God.

—Romans 10:17

And take the helmet of salvation, and the sword of the Spirit, which is the word of God.

—EPHESIANS 6:17

The grass withers, the flower fades, But the word of our God stands forever.

—ISAIAH 40:8

...having been born again, not of corruptible seed but incorruptible, through the word of God which lives and abides forever...

—I PETER 1:23 (NKJV)

But He said, "More than that, blessed are those who hear the word of God and keep it."

—LUKE 11:28 (NKJV)

He was clothed with a robe dipped in blood, and His name is called The Word of God.

—REVELATION 19:13 (NKJV)

...for which I suffer trouble as an evildoer, even to the point of chains; but the word of God is not chained.

—II TIMOTHY 2:9 (NKJV)

The Struggle to Believe

*I*f I were to tell you that believing in God is easy, I'd be dishonest. The truth is, it's not, and I believe that it's not supposed to be. It is rewarding without measure, but it's not easy.

The world that we live in today is filled with corruption and dismay. I'm old enough to recognize what was and what is. There's a huge difference in our world now compared to what it was when I was a kid. The Internet smacks you in the face every chance it gets and gives you its take on life. Sometimes you'll find good and sometimes you'll find evil. Our world is covered in a heavy coating of evil.

However, when you walk with God and believe in him with all of your heart, you're different than those who have not chosen this path. You are in this world, but not of it. Think long and hard about that. You are *in* this world, but not *of* it. Once you become a born-again your spirit will recognize this. Always remember the enemy doesn't want you to believe in God. Your shield is that of the Lord.

After these things the word of the Lord came to Abram in a vision, saying, "Do not fear, Abram, I am a shield to you; your reward shall be very great."

—GENESIS 15:1

The grass withers, the flower fades, but the word of our God will stand for ever.

—ISAIAH 40:8

Jesus replied, "With all the earnestness I possess I tell you this: Unless you are born again, you can never get into the Kingdom of God."

—JOHN 3

You might read that scripture and ask yourself *why?* I'm sure that I did before becoming a born-again. In fact I know that the thought never crossed my mind. I thought that I'd go to heaven because I went to church and believed. The Bible clearly states that not all will go to heaven. You enter heaven by forgiveness and through the righteousness that Jesus gives you. You do not enter into heaven by the Christian life.

"Today, you will be with me in paradise."

—LUKE 23:43

For it is by grace you have been saved, through faith—and this not from yourselves, it is the gift of God—not by works, so that no one can boast.

—Ephesians 2:8-9

Because, if you confess with your mouth that Jesus is Lord and believe in your heart that God raised him from the dead, you will be saved.

—Romans 10:9

"Not everyone who says to me, 'Lord, Lord,' will enter the kingdom of heaven, but the one who does the will of my Father who is in heaven. On that day many will say to me, 'Lord, Lord, did we not prophesy in your name, and cast out demons in your name, and do many mighty works in your name?' And then will I declare to them, 'I never knew you; depart from me, you workers of lawlessness.' "Everyone then who hears these words of mine and does them will be like a wise man who built his house on the rock. And the rain fell, and the floods came, and the winds blew and beat on that house, but it did not fall, because it had been founded on the rock."

—Matthew 7:21-27

For the wages of sin is death, but the free gift of God is eternal life in Christ Jesus our Lord.

—Romans 6:23

Jesus answered him, "Truly, truly, I say to you, unless one is born again he cannot see the kingdom of God."

—JOHN 3:3

Think about John 3:3 for just one moment. I really feel like that needs to be said one more time: *God places you in the right circumstances and places, always.* There is a catch. You must be a born-again Christian to fully understand what I just told you.

I'm not being a snobbish Christian, but I'm an honest one. When you transform into a born-again believer, you're not the same person that you were. This sounds crazy to a non-believer, I know, and the ridicule and judgment that one receives once they become a born-again is constant. I'm just warning you.

We live in an upside-down world, and your born-again spirit is always right-side up. Sunny side up that is! It's important that you don't lose sight of that. Knowing that a new, different person has replaced the old is exciting. The things that you were once attracted to seem to be uninteresting after you become a born-again.

And without faith it is impossible to please God, because anyone who comes to Him must believe that he exists and that He rewards those who earnestly seek Him.

—HEBREWS 11:6

I Thought That
I Was a Christian

*T*hroughout most of my life I've taken pride in telling myself that I was a good person. It wasn't until I asked God into my heart, though, and recited the sinner's prayer, that the Holy Spirit changed me. Isn't that interesting how I went to church, practiced treating others the way that I wished to be treated, but was truly not a real Christian?

It's not complicated being a real Christian, but it's not easy. The Holy Spirit helps you to realize things that you've never realized before once you do. You require the assistance of the Holy Spirit for this amazing transformation to take place. Having the ability to distinguish a casual relationship with God and a stick-to-your-bones spiritual one is comparable to the difference of night and day or a rainy cloudy day and a sunshiny bright one. You won't understand or see it until you become a born-again.

It seems so simple asking God to come into your heart

and forgive you of your sins. Who would ever imagine that saying those words would change you into a different person? I know that I didn't even come close to understanding until I repeated the sinner's prayer. I'm telling you this because you may be like I was before I became a born-again Christian and think that you're on the right track. I want you to experience life with this glorious gift and lifestyle change like I did. My amazing transformation was beyond anything that I've ever experienced. There's no drug or alcohol high that could even come close to the soulful and supernatural high of being a born-again!

The Sinner's Prayer:
Dear Lord Jesus, I know that I am a sinner, and I ask for your forgiveness. I believe you died for my sins and rose from the dead. I turn from my sins and invite you to come into my heart and life. I want to trust and follow you as my Lord and Savior.

If you said that simple prayer my friend, you're now a born-again Christian. Congratulations seem insignificant on something so magnificent! Share your transformation with friends and family. Some will be happy for you and others will be confused and not understand. You, however, will feel the enormous power of God take over your spirit. As the days and weeks pass, it's important to study the Bible and take up the sword of God. Each new day will present a better understanding of the love that God has for you, and your transformation will grow and cultivate as you study the Bible and trust in God for everything.

Walking with Jesus

*A*fter you surrender your heart to God and say that simple but powerful prayer, you are about to embrace a life like you've never had—a life filled with joy and peace, regardless of the situation. In fact, your spirit will be transformed.

The reason this happens is because once you accept Christ, he supernaturally comes to live inside you. Before I was a born-again Christian I could not say that, but now that I'm joined with the Holy Spirit, I can happily shout it to the hills! Until you become a born-again Christian you won't understand or comprehend this.

I'm guessing, but I'd imagine that God's perfect love is wrapped also in a perfect plan. Once you say that prayer and repeat it with sincerity, you are part of God's perfect plan and your future is bright. You are going to live forever!

You might wonder what's next. I can't specifically

answer that question, because once you ask God into your heart by saying that prayer you will be directed by God on the path that he has just for you. You will immediately realize that this path is different than any other you've ever walked on. You'll worry for nothing as you turn over your troubles and heartache to God. Miracles will come as you walk with faith.

It's not going to happen just like that. It will require some work from you. This so-called work is not what you're probably thinking. This work will be to study Jesus and read the Bible. I can promise you that if you stay in the word, and pray over each and every situation, that God will handle things with his perfect love. This love is unlike any other worldly love. You will recognize it as such as you grow in faith.

We talked about the good, and now it's time to talk about the bad. Just as there is light, there is darkness. The enemy will sneak around and come at you with all that he's got once you become a born-again, but you possess the most powerful weapon against him—your love for the Lord.

The Bible plainly states that Satan comes to steal, kill, and destroy. He never really had to worry about you before you became a born-again believer, your human behavior and hollow spirit fit into his plan for you. But once you became a born-again everything changed not only for you, but for Satan as well.

I've learned through my faith and trust that life continues around me, but there's a gigantic difference that dwells in my spirit and that is unlike anything I've ever experienced. Bad things happen, death, destruction, and even despair, but my heart is filled with the Holy Spirit and peace and joy regardless of what comes my way! Who doesn't want that?

I didn't realize that I was missing anything in my life. I had the perfect family, job, and everything that I wanted, but when I repeated that prayer, it hit me just how little I had, and that I wasn't benefiting from the true gifts that God had for me, both on earth and in heaven.

I probably sound redundant as I share my story, but it's important to remember these things as they will help you to be strong and faithful to God. You will fall, but you will get up. After you fall, ask God for forgiveness and repent. He's the perfect father. All-knowing and filled with an amazing forgiveness and love. He will pick you up and nurture your heart the way he only can do. He's God!

And no wonder, for even Satan disguises himself as an angel of light.

—2 CORINTHIANS 11:14

In their case the god of this world has blinded the minds of the unbelievers, to keep them from seeing the light of the gospel of the glory of Christ, who is the image of God.

—2 CORINTHIANS 4:4

Submit yourselves therefore to God. Resist the devil, and he will flee from you.

—JAMES 4:7

The God of peace will soon crush Satan under your feet. The grace of our Lord Jesus Christ be with you.

—ROMANS 16:20

Put on the whole armor of God, that you may be able to stand against the schemes of the devil.

—EPHESIANS 6:11

The thief comes only to steal and kill and destroy. I came that they may have life and have it abundantly.

—JOHN 10:10

But he turned and said to Peter, "Get behind me, Satan! You are a hindrance to me. For you are not setting your mind on the things of God, but on the things of man."

—MATTHEW 16:23

For we do not wrestle against flesh and blood, but against the rulers, against the authorities, against the cosmic powers over this present darkness, against the spiritual forces of evil in the heavenly places.

—EPHESIANS 6:12

And the devil who had deceived them was thrown into the lake of fire and sulfur where the beast and the false prophet were, and they will be tormented day and night forever and ever.

—REVELATION 20:10

Be sober-minded; be watchful. Your adversary the devil prowls around like a roaring lion, seeking someone to devour. Resist him, firm in your faith, knowing that the same kinds of suffering are being experienced by your brotherhood throughout the world.

—1 PETER 5:8-9

And he seized the dragon, that ancient serpent, who is the devil and Satan, and bound him for a thousand years,

—REVELATION 20:2

Jesus answered him, "Truly, truly, I say to you, unless one is born again he cannot see the kingdom of God."

—JOHN 3:3

For the wages of sin is death, but the free gift of God is eternal life in Christ Jesus our Lord.

—ROMANS 6:23

Do not marvel that I said to you, 'You must be born again.'

—JOHN 3:7

Jesus answered, "Truly, truly, I say to you, unless one is born of water and the Spirit, he cannot enter the kingdom of God."

—JOHN 3:5

He saved us, not because of works done by us in righteousness, but according to his own mercy, by the washing of regeneration and renewal of the Holy Spirit.

—TITUS 3:5

The wind blows where it wishes, and you hear its sound, but you do not know where it comes from or where it goes. So it is with everyone who is born of the Spirit.

—JOHN 3:8

That which is born of the flesh is flesh, and that which is born of the Spirit is spirit.

—JOHN 3:6

Wow factor!

I am thinking that by the time you read this you've surrendered your heart to God and have repeated that special prayer. The angels are rejoicing and await your arrival to heaven when it's your time. Meanwhile, God is watching over you and blessing you each and every day here on earth. The moment that you take your last breath is the moment that you'll begin an eternity with God. An eternity! Forever and ever!

"Truly, truly, I say to you, whoever hears my word and believes him who sent me has eternal life. He does not come into judgment, but has passed from death to life."

—JOHN 5:24

"This is the bread that comes down from heaven, so that one may eat of it and not die. I am the living bread that came down from heaven. If anyone eats of this bread, he will live

forever. And the bread that I will give for the life of the world is my flesh." The Jews then disputed among themselves, saying, "How can this man give us his flesh to eat?" So Jesus said to them, "Truly, truly, I say to you, unless you eat the flesh of the Son of Man and drink his blood, you have no life in you. Whoever feeds on my flesh and drinks my blood has eternal life, and I will raise him up on the last day..."

—John 6:50-71

"In my Father's house are many rooms. If it were not so, would I have told you that I go to prepare a place for you? And if I go and prepare a place for you, I will come again and will take you to myself, that where I am you may be also."

—John 14:2-3

"And if your hand causes you to sin, cut it off. It is better for you to enter life crippled than with two hands to go to hell, to the unquenchable fire. And if your foot causes you to sin, cut it off. It is better for you to enter life lame than with two feet to be thrown into hell. And if your eye causes you to sin, tear it out. It is better for you to enter the kingdom of God with one eye than with two eyes to be thrown into hell, 'where their worm does not die and the fire is not quenched.'"

—Matthew 5:29-32

So we do not lose heart. Though our outer self is wasting away, our inner self is being renewed day by day. For this light momentary affliction is preparing for us an eternal weight of glory beyond all comparison, as we look not to the things that are seen but to the things that are unseen. For the things that are seen are transient, but the things that are unseen are eternal.

—2 CORINTHIANS 4:16-18

"Enter by the narrow gate. For the gate is wide and the way is easy that leads to destruction, and those who enter by it are many. For the gate is narrow and the way is hard that leads to life, and those who find it are few."

—MATTHEW 7:13-14

Fight the good fight of the faith. Take hold of the eternal life to which you were called and about which you made the good confession in the presence of many witnesses.

—1 TIMOTHY 6:12

Living the Good Life

You've heard that phrase before. I would imagine there are numerous interpretations, but for me there's only one true good life, and in fact, I would call it a great life when Christ is center stage!

This life I speak of is easily obtained, but few actually live it. It's the life of a saved human. Some are on the path to discover it, while others are apprehensive and doubtful. Some don't believe that it's important, and others feel that it doesn't exist. It simply sounds too far-fetched for them to believe. My only regret in life is that I didn't call to Jesus when I was young, as I realize now that this great life cannot exist without the power of the Almighty. It just can't. You might believe that it can, but it just won't work.

The happiness and joy that one receives being a saved person is unlike anything that I've ever experienced. It's the closest you'll get to heaven until you get there! You walk on earth being filled with the Holy Spirit. I believe that I need to repeat that last sentence. You walk on earth while being filled with the Holy Spirit! You're still you, but your spirit has been transformed into a super size!

When I ponder those thoughts, I can't help but feel happy. My heart is filled with God's joy and peace. Those feelings are surrounded with the same joy and peace that Jesus had when he walked here on earth. It's the biggest life transformation that you'll ever have!

Well, with the exception of your next life that never ends. This by the way comes automatically once you accept Jesus and make him your Lord and Savior. No need to pass go, you're headed down the path that was designed specifically for you by God. There will be bumps in the road, even landslides, but your faith and trust will allow you to overcome what lies ahead. Your spirit and soul are filled with a healthy dose of love and understanding.

The wealthiest person in the world can never exceed or compare to the wealth that you now have in understanding Christ. As you walk with him and talk with him and read the Bible you grow to become who God intended you to be. He loves you so much and puts great value on your salvation. He has written your name in the Book of Life. This is a life that never ends. One that makes this life feel like the blink of an eye. When I take time to really think about that, my faith becomes stronger.

Coming from a
Good Place

*T*here are many times that I ask myself if I'm coming from a good place. *Could the words that come from my mouth offend someone?* When you are transformed with a born-again spirit, you become more aware of what you say and how you say it.

These changes come from a loving understanding that each of us is going through something and that a loving hug or kind word can offer a soothing assurance that someone cares. Now more than ever it's important to treat others with kindness.

On the other side of the spectrum, it's also important to stand up for what you believe. Keep in mind that not everyone believes what you believe, and they will not be responsive to your spiritual way of thinking. Knowing that, the chance that you're going to offend someone is ever-present, especially in today's society. This is a work-in-progress that evolves back and forth and up and down.

I have discovered that prayer and reaching out to God for understanding and solutions is always my best defense against vengeful comments or malicious humans. We're all going to encounter situations that present emotions that sometimes interfere with our walk with God. We are human! Keep the faith, and never lose sight of the fact that God has it under control.

When these tests come into your life they aren't from God. They are from Satan. Living my life with this understanding has changed my old perspective to a healthy productive one. One of the perks of being a Christ-follower is that it's easier for you to stay humble and true to God's love that he has freely given to you.

As you grow in faith and trust in the Holy Spirit through prayer and reading his word, you will also grow in understanding of why people do what they do. What I have discovered through God's teachings is that sometimes hurt people hurt others. When you recognize hurt you tend to not let it get under your skin.

The evil one is on constant alert to tear you away from your walk with the Lord, and he will stop at nothing to do that. He will send malice, hate, and evil in the forms of other humans. I've witnessed both hate and revenge in my personal life and in my business, but I have learned and continue to learn that there is nothing your earthly carnal body can do to change the situation. Turn it over to God and he will work miracles with your hardships and challenges. Your heart should be forgiving, always.

So when you recognize these unfortunate situations with non-believers you will start to understand where their origin is. Once you realize these strangers in the night come to steal, kill, and destroy and are instructed from Satan, you have a better chance of combating it.

The more you open up your Bible and read his word, the more powerful your sword. The more you pray and believe, the more powerful your sword. Your defense comes from the Almighty himself. As a born-again believer you have the power of Christ living in you. It's important that you never lose sight of this truth.

I believe that these tests are part of your journey, and that without them you might not feel the need to trust in God. Think about how God sent his only Son to the cross and how he died for us. Jesus dying on the cross is the central truth of the Bible. The entire Bible revolves around this powerful truth: Jesus died for you so that you could have eternal life. Your sins are forgiven once you call upon Christ to fill your heart with his love. As he was brutally nailed to that cross, dying a slow and painful death, he says, *it is finished!* Those are the most powerful words in the Bible! God sacrificed his only Son for all of humanity.

For whosoever shall call upon the name of the Lord shall be saved. How then shall they call on him in whom they have not believed? And how shall they believe in him of whom they have not heard? And how shall they hear without a preacher?

—ROMANS 10:13-15 (KJV)

The Holy Spirit

*B*ecause I am a born again, I'm also filled with the Holy Spirit. You're probably asking what that means. I, for one, had no idea until it happened to me.

When I don't stay in the word it goes away. I'm not sure how it works, but it seems to be a channel that connects you with God when you do stay in the word as you read the Bible. It kind of feels like there is a string attached to my spirit and God's, and when I don't stay in his word, it doesn't completely go away, but it's weak compared to when I stay in the word and out of this world.

That might sound kind of crazy, especially if you haven't turned your heart over to God. I'm thinking by the time that you get to this chapter you've considered doing that or you've already asked Jesus to come into your life. You've repeated his simple prayer. I say his prayer, because it's very much God's desire that one day you hang out with Jesus and his father. I can't imagine a life of pure love surrounded by such holy beings, but my imagination allows me to ponder it. No matter how much I imagine it will be, my earthly mind can't grasp it. I guess if we all knew how to play the game of life and the afterlife we might participate, but we might not. Believing in something that you can't see or hear or feel is a challenge for some, but once you turn your spirit over to God you'll completely understand what I'm saying. As I walk with the Lord, my faith expands and grows through his grace. Not my grace, but his grace. God!

When Elizabeth heard Mary's greeting, the baby leaped in her womb; and Elizabeth was filled with the Holy Spirit.

—LUKE 1:41

So Ananias departed and entered the house, and after laying his hands on him said, "Brother Saul, the Lord Jesus, who appeared to you on the road by which you were coming, has sent me so that you may regain your sight and be filled with the Holy Spirit."

—ACTS 9:17

I have filled him with the Spirit of God in wisdom, in understanding, in knowledge, and in all kinds of craftsmanship,

—EXODUS 31:3

I refer to being filled with the Holy Spirit as a super power from God. You begin to feel the Lord inside you. When you call upon the Lord to fill you with the Holy Spirit, you're going to feel it! You only need to ask God to fill you. Once you're saved, you're on the path to also be filled with the Holy Spirit. It's unlike anything you'll ever encounter! Your love for Christ grows and becomes supernaturally powerful!

On the other hand I am filled with power—
With the Spirit of the Lord—
And with justice and courage
To make known to Jacob his rebellious act,
Even to Israel his sin.

—Micah 3:8

Once I became filled with the Holy Spirit, my life changed. My trust has been cultivated and nourished in ways that I could never imagine existed. His Spirit is most evident sometimes in our trials and tribulations. His power supernaturally fills our hearts and transforms us into his image. It's a life journey and a growth experience that I can honestly say is the most significant thing that's ever happened to me. I have experienced a huge difference as a born-again believer after being filled with the Holy Spirit.

So Ananias departed and entered the house, and after laying his hands on him said, "Brother Saul, the Lord Jesus, who appeared to you on the road by which you were coming, has sent me so that you may regain your sight and be filled with the Holy Spirit."

—ACTS 9:17

And they were all filled with the Holy Spirit and began to speak with other tongues, as the Spirit was giving them utterance.

—ACTS 2:4

And when they had prayed, the place where they had gathered together was shaken, and they were all filled with the Holy Spirit and began to speak the word of God with boldness.

—ACTS 4:31

Reading Proverbs

*T*he Bible is filled with powerful knowledge. When I read Proverbs I'm reminded of how God shared the truths of life. Typically those words are stern and potent. It makes sense to me that they would be, because how else is God going to get through to stubborn prideful people like me?

Did you know that God personalizes the way that he teaches you and blesses you? It makes logical sense that he would. He did create you. He knows what you're going to do before you actually do it. He's an all-knowing God. The Bible tells us this.

The eyes of the LORD are in every place, beholding the evil and the good.

—PROVERBS 15:3

The LORD hates the gifts of the wicked, but delights in the prayers of his people.

—PROVERBS 15:8

The rich and the poor are alike before the LORD, who made them all.

—PROVERBS 22:2

Teach a child to choose the right path, and when he is older, he will remain upon it.

—PROVERBS 22:6

Lasting Effects

I remember it as though it was yesterday. When I was seventeen, my boyfriend and I went out to dinner with another couple. I wasn't old enough to drink, but they were. I don't recall just how much the other three drank that night, all I remember is that on the way home, my boyfriend asked if the other guy wanted to drive. He said yes, and no sooner than he got behind the wheel he began swaying the car back and forth on the interstate.

My boyfriend asked him to stop, but he kept going back and forth, in and out along the highway. Next thing I knew the car was rolling and I was being tossed around like a rag-doll. I felt shoes hitting me in the face, and sharp metal stuck in my body as the car whipped over and over. Then as the car was turning over I had a vision. It all happened so fast, but yet seemed to be moving in slow motion. I remember seeing my body dead under the car, just laying there. The exact clothes I was wearing and my eyes shut, and I knew that I was dead. At that moment I shout-ed, *God I don't want to die*. In that instant the car stopped. It was upside down and most of the windows were broken out. We crawled out the window into the winter night and realized that the driver's wife was not around. She had been thrown onto the other side of the highway.

Shortly after the wreck, the ambulance arrived, along with a state trooper. He told us that he couldn't believe that any of us had survived as the car appeared to have turned at least five times. The girl who was thrown out ended up being in a body cast for over a year, and she was never able to fully recover. I had a gash in my wrist, where I remember holding my hands over my face, and a sharp piece of metal from the car pierced my wrist. The horrible car accident had lasting effects on my life.

Although I was not a born-again at the time, I'll never forget that vision and how I shouted out to God to save me. He did! For whatever reason, he did. I refer to this in-cident as one of my miracles. This is one of many miracles that I've experienced in my life. I've always been forever grateful to God for saving me from death on that cold winter night.

The trooper drove us home and when I went inside I realized that I was covered with blood. I'll never forget that I was wearing green. My dad had me remove my pants and shirt, and he soaked them in cold water to remove the blood. I remember each and every little moment during that wreck and after. The kindness of the trooper, my boyfriend's concern for my safety, and my dad's loving kindness. But most of all, I remember how I came so very close to death and God saved me.

We each have similar stories about how God rescued us or saved us from a dire situation. Some believe it's fate, while others don't believe in anything. I knew then, as I know now, even though I was not a believer at the time, that God spared my life.

My past has been filled with numerous miracles, and I realize now that each of them has led me on a path of understanding more of God. My journey continues as I take up the book of God with a yearning to understand God's word.

He has high hopes and dreams for his children. Whether you believe or not, he hopes you will, and that you'll spend an eternity with both the Son and the Father in heaven. As I look at the craziness that's in our world, and the evil that surrounds us, I feel now more than ever that we need a Savior. I go about my life just like most other people do, except I've come to realize that this is not my home. My real home is with Jesus. A born-again believer is in this world, but not of it. The more I stop and think about those words the more I understand God's design, and it comforts me each and every day.

Creatures Big and Small

When I think of God, my mind automatically thinks that he's the smartest being in the universe. After all, he created it and all of its inhabitants.

Sometimes when I slow down and take a walk through a garden or forest I'm reminded of just how amazing God really is. From the creatures that walk this earth, the green grass, the blue sky, and all of earth's creation, all of which have been magically designed by God. It's incredible for me to fathom those thoughts.

Sometimes I smile and say out loud, *thank you God for all things*. Like the clean water that I drink, the warm home when it's cold, and the many blessings that you've brought my way. These somewhat simple things all come from God, and when I lose sight of these grateful thoughts, my heart does not feel whole.

You probably recognize when your heart doesn't feel whole. Everything can be going right, but there's a tugging or feeling that something just isn't complete. Something is missing. When I have those feelings, they're usually wrapped around less time with God and more time in the world. It's a reminder that I need to spend more time with God. Without fail, each time that this happens and I fill my soul with God's word, I come back.

This is a normal thing that happens when you become a born-again. Your faith and trust and devotion to God become crucial to your well-being. It's as though your spirit is on automatic pilot, because it recognizes when you're not fully filling your heart and expanding your understanding and knowledge of God.

You are also putting on the shield of God. You need his protection against the evils of the world. This is important especially as you live in the world today. I, for one, need all the help that I can get. The darkness that fills this world seems to grow each day. It's important that we're the light, and the way that you stay in the light is in walking with the Lord.

What, then, shall we say in response to these things? If God is for us, who can be against us?

—ROMANS 8:28-39

The LORD is my light and my salvation— whom shall I fear? The LORD is the stronghold of my life— of whom shall I be afraid?

When the wicked advance against me to devour me, it is my enemies and my foes who will stumble and fall. Though an army besiege me, my heart will not fear; though war break out against me, even then I will be confident. One thing I ask from the LORD, this only do I seek: that I may dwell in the house of the LORD all the days of my life, to gaze on the beauty of the LORD and to seek him in his temple.

For in the day of trouble he will keep me safe in his dwelling; he will hide me in the shelter of his sacred tent and set me high upon a rock. Then my head will be exalted above the enemies who surround me; at his sacred tent I will sacrifice with shouts of joy; I will sing and make music to the LORD.

Hear my voice when I call, LORD; be merciful to me and answer me. My heart says of you, "Seek his face!" Your face, LORD, I will seek. Do not hide your face from me, do not turn your servant away in anger; you have been my helper. Do not reject me or forsake me, God my Savior. Though my father and mother forsake me, the LORD will receive me.

Teach me your way, LORD; lead me in a straight path because of my oppressors. Do not turn me over to the desire of my foes, for false witnesses rise up against me, spouting malicious accusations. I remain confident of this: I will see the goodness of the LORD in the land of the living.

Wait for the LORD; be strong and take heart and wait for the LORD.

—PSALMS 27

You're going to have challenging times. I've discovered that since becoming a born-again most of my challenges have come from other humans. It's important that you stay in the light, and remain gentle and kind. Remember you are an example, and a child of God. You are God's ambassador. That's a tough pill to swallow!

There's a lot of pressure that's associated with being a born-again believer. Your life should be an example and teach others about God's love for them. Stand up for what you believe in, and never allow a situation or other person to pull you away from God. He is the most important person in your life. His love for you exceeds all earthly love. In fact, his love for you is a love above all loves. It's also an everlasting love that remains forever. You are a follower of Christ and he lives in you.

When you become a believer you now have authority with his word. When bad things come, you have authority to remove them or are able to prevent the situation from overcoming you. Make sure your prayers are strong with faith and that you say them with authority.

Whoever dwells in the shelter of the Most High will rest in the shadow of the Almighty. I will say of the LORD, "He is my refuge and my fortress, my God, in whom I trust." Surely he will save you from the fowler's snare and from the deadly pestilence. He will cover you with his feathers, and under his wings you will find refuge; his faithfulness will be your shield and rampart. You will not fear the terror of night, nor the arrow that flies by day, nor the pestilence that stalks in the darkness, nor the plague that destroys at midday. A thousand may fall at your side, ten thousand at your right hand, but it will not come near you. You will only observe with your eyes and see the punishment of the wicked. If you say, "The LORD is my refuge," and you make the Most High your dwelling, no harm will overtake you, no disaster will come near your tent. For he will command his angels concerning you to guard you in all your ways; they will lift you up in their hands, so that you will not strike your foot against a stone. You will tread on the lion and the cobra; you will trample the great lion and the serpent. "Because he loves me," says the LORD, "I will rescue him; I will protect him, for he acknowledges my name. He will call on me, and I will answer him; I will be with him in trouble, I will deliver him and honor him. With long life I will satisfy him and show him my salvation."

—PSALMS 91

It's important that you believe in your words and prayers. Your words are powerful and strong. Nowadays people's words aren't what they once were. When I was young, if a person gave you their word, it was as though you signed a contract. In this day, and not all of the time, but most of the time, a person's word is not really their word. It's not important to them to follow through with their words.

It's not like that with God. He hears all of your words and he honors them. That is why he hears our prayers. Our words are powerful! Remember that your word is strong in God's name. In other words, train your mind to think about your words. Think before you speak. Don't use discouraging words, but instead practice encouraging ones. Those are the words that come from God.

God will never give you negative or discouraging words. With God, your talk stands behind the walk! Talk the talk that is founded on God's word. It's the true word. Take authority over your words. Use your words with caution. I once read: *the words you speak become the house you live in.* There is a lot of truth to that phrase.

We all stumble in many ways. Anyone who is never at fault in what they say is perfect, able to keep their whole body in check. When we put bits into the mouths of horses to make them obey us, we can turn the whole animal. Or take ships as an example. Although they are so large and are driven by strong winds, they are steered by a very small rudder wherever the pilot wants to go. Likewise, the tongue is a small part of the body, but it makes great boasts. Consider what a great forest is set on fire by a small spark. The tongue also is a fire, a world of evil among the parts of the body. It corrupts the whole body, sets the whole course of one's life on fire, and is itself set on fire by hell. All kinds of animals, birds, reptiles and sea creatures are being tamed and have been tamed by mankind, but no human being can tame the tongue. It is a restless evil, full of deadly poison. With the tongue we praise our Lord and Father, and with it we curse human beings, who have been made in God's likeness. Out of the same mouth come praise and cursing. My brothers and sisters, this should not be. Can both fresh water and salt water flow from the same spring? My brothers and sisters, can a fig tree bear olives, or a grapevine bear figs? Neither can a salt spring produce fresh water.

—JAMES 3

A Woman of Faith

 W hat exactly does it mean to be a woman of faith? It means that you believe in God's word and you always trust in him for all things. It means that life is filled with ups and downs and death and even despair, but your faith always overrides doubt and negative forces. You are a child of God, and by declaring this, you are now released from fear, doubt, and whatever comes your way. Your faith is built from trust and vice versa. You are unstoppable in your faith.

Now I understand why some preachers yell their sermons! He lives in you, and his angels watch over you. We need to remember that when we turn our heart over to God that this is truth. We may not understand it, but it's as true as blue. You have chosen to be born-again. You are no longer the person you were. You are a new construction, made by God. He has washed you clean of your sins.

When I began writing this book, it was apparent that

some would not agree or believe like I do. That's okay, but if there's one person who turns his or her heart over to God completely, I'm content to have written this book! It will be the biggest gift that I've ever received.

My hope is that you will grow in your faith and desire to learn more about the Father and his Son. It's one of the most beautiful love stories ever! I do everything to live life the way God would expect me to. It's not easy. Each day is filled with challenges and disappointments, but I turn to God especially during those difficult times, trusting that his plans are best.

I hope that you will explore God's word by reading the Bible. It's a powerful book filled with life answers. Before I became a born-again believer, the Bible seldom made sense when I read it. Now that I've surrendered and confessed my many sins, the words and content touch my heart and soul in ways that I could never imagine. Both the Old and New Testaments are powerful reading that I feel blessed to have available.

Keep the faith, and trust in him for everything. I promise you that he will protect you with his almighty love and understanding. He is a God of forgiveness and love.

May God's peace fill your heart and the joy that comes from only him consume your life.

She surveys a field and acquires it; from her own resources, she plants a vineyard. She works energetically; her arms are powerful.

—PROVERBS 31:16-17

"I've commanded you to be brave and strong, haven't I? Don't be alarmed or terrified, because the Lord your God is with you wherever you go."

—JOSHUA 1:9

Don't try to make yourselves beautiful on the outside, with stylish hair or by wearing gold jewelry or fine clothes. Instead, make yourselves beautiful on the inside, in your hearts, with the enduring quality of a gentle, peaceful spirit. This type of beauty is very precious in God's eyes.

—1 PETER 3:3-4

"Happy is she who believed that the Lord would fulfill the promises he made to her."

—LUKE 1:45

Strength and honor are her clothing; she is confident about the future.

—PROVERBS 31:25

My Beautiful Faith

I am a born-again believer, and there's nothing that has ever been compared to this supernatural experience.

My faith is my fortress! No matter what comes my way and regardless of the severity of the circumstance, I always have joy in my soul for one reason, and one reason only, my faith!

I've been both wealthy and poor. I searched for happiness until I could search no more, and reached for things that were unreachable. I've experienced love and hate simultaneously. My only regret is that I wish I'd called upon Jesus many years ago. I had no idea the impact he would have on my life!

Each of us is searching for peace in our lives, but very few achieve it. That golden moment when you let God take the reins is a moment that you'll never forget. Your heart will be filled with the glory of God, and you'll never be the same again. You'll start to notice a positive difference in the way that you react and treat others. You're the same person, but you're an improved version. Not within your eyes but God's eyes. The angels rejoiced the day that you accepted your salvation.

But didn't he earn his right to heaven by all the good things he did? No, for being saved is a gift; if a person could earn it by being good, then it wouldn't be free—but it is! It is given to those who do not work for it. For God declares sinners to be good in his sight if they have faith in Christ to save them from God's wrath.

—Romans 4:4-5

Jesus replied, "With all the earnestness I possess I tell you this: Unless you are born again, you can never get into the Kingdom of God."

—John 3:3

Oh, my children, how you are hurting me! I am once again suffering for you the pains of a mother waiting for her child to be born—longing for the time when you will finally be filled with Christ.

—Galatians 4:19

All honor to God, the God and Father of our Lord Jesus Christ; for it is his boundless mercy that has given us the priv-

ilege of being born again so that we are now members of God's own family. Now we live in the hope of eternal life because Christ rose again from the dead.

—1 PETER 1:3

The person who has been born into God's family does not make a practice of sinning because now God's life is in him; so he can't keep on sinning, for this new life has been born into him and controls him—he has been born again.

—1 JOHN 3:9

This last verse is one of my favorites as it touches on how once you're born again you experience a new life.

Don't ever forget those wonderful days when you first learned about Christ. Remember how you kept right on with the Lord even though it meant terrible suffering. Sometimes you were laughed at and beaten, and sometimes you watched and sympathized with others suffering the same things. You suffered with those thrown into jail, and you were actually joyful when all you owned was taken from you, knowing that better things were awaiting you in heaven, things that would be yours forever.

—HEBREWS 10:32

Faith is the substance of things hoped for.

JILL MCDOWELL is a fourth generation soap maker who resides in Middle America where she sells her soap and sundries at her modern apothecary shop. Her faith journey has been molded and nourished by the customers that frequent her shop and the strangers that visit from afar. Since 1997 she's been refining her craft and sharpening her knowledge of operating a small business through her faith. She gives the glory to God for her success and attributes her life's happiness to her faith. Through the ups and downs, she's come to realize that faith matures through the trials of life, and that with each obstacle comes a better understanding of God's perfect plan. She's encouraged and strengthened by reading the Bible, and energized by those who share their faith.